IS-921.A: Implementing Critical Infrastructure Security and Resilience

By

Fema

11/1/2013

Lesson 1: Introduction and Planning

Course Welcome

The purpose of this course is to introduce those with critical infrastructure security and resilience duties and responsibilities to the information and the resources available to them in the execution of the mission to protect and improve resilience in the Nation's critical infrastructure.

Course Objectives

At the end of this course, you should be able to:

- Summarize critical infrastructure responsibilities.
- Identify the range of critical infrastructure security and resilience activities conducted by government and private-sector partners at the Federal, State, local, tribal, territorial, and regional levels.
- Describe processes for effective information sharing with critical infrastructure partners.
- Identify various methods for assessing and validating information.
- Describe how a risk management process is used to identify vulnerabilities and to manage risks.
- Identify effective practices for critical infrastructure planning to apply at the State, local, tribal, territorial, and regional levels.
- Describe alternatives for integrating critical infrastructure considerations and protective measures into continuity, emergency management, emergency operations, and other existing plans.

Lesson Overview

This lesson presents an overview of critical infrastructure roles and responsibilities.

Upon completing this lesson, you should be able to:

- Summarize key critical infrastructure responsibilities at the Federal, State, local, tribal, territorial, and regional levels.
- Identify potential critical infrastructure security and resilience planning activities.
- Identify the broad categories that should be addressed in critical infrastructure security and resilience plans and programs.

The National Infrastructure Protection Plan

Our national security and standard of living depend on the reliable functioning of our critical infrastructure. Critical infrastructure includes a vast array of assets, networks, and systems such as food, water, energy, communications, transportation, banking, and more.

The incapacitation or destruction of our critical infrastructure would have a debilitating impact on security, the national economy, or public health and safety. Collectively, our infrastructure sectors provide the underpinnings of our economy and our society.

The risks we face as a Nation are complex. They include a mix of human-caused and naturally occurring threats and hazards that range from terrorist attacks, cyber threats, oil spills, and power outages due to hurricanes, earthquakes, floods, tornadoes, and wildfires.

The complex interdependencies and physical characteristics of our infrastructure make it essential that we identify and mitigate vulnerabilities. Ensuring the continued operation of our infrastructure requires a strategy that achieves resilience so that regardless of the threats electricity flows; communications remain robust; and planes, trains, and buses continue to operate.

Resilience is defined as our ability to resist, absorb, recover from, or successfully adapt to adversity or disruption. We must be able to maintain critical operations and functions in the face of a crisis; prepare for, respond to, and manage a crisis or disruption as it unfolds; and return to and reconstitute normal operations quickly and efficiently.

Security and resilience complement each other and are both necessary elements of a comprehensive risk management strategy. Protecting and ensuring the resilience of our infrastructure is a shared responsibility that involves all levels of government in partnership with owners and operators.

The National Infrastructure Protection Plan, or NIPP, provides a framework for partnerships that enhances critical infrastructure security and resilience and helps build a safer, more secure, and more resilient America.

Together, we can enhance critical infrastructure security and resilience.

Critical Infrastructure

Critical infrastructure includes the physical or virtual assets, systems, and networks that are so vital to the United States that their incapacitation or destruction would have a debilitating impact on security, the national economy, or public health and safety.

The vast majority of the critical infrastructure in our country is owned and operated by the private sector. For that reason, partnerships with public and private sector owners and operators are critical.

National Infrastructure Protection Plan

The National Infrastructure Protection Plan (NIPP) provides the unifying structure for the integration of critical infrastructure security efforts and resilience strategies into a single national program.

The NIPP formalizes and strengthens existing critical infrastructure partnerships and creates the baseline for how the public and private sectors will work together.

NIPP 2013: *Partnering for Critical Infrastructure Security and Resilience* includes a whole-community approach to risk management and a shared vision to ensure physical and cyber critical infrastructure remains secure and resilient, essential services and resources are available in the face of emergencies, and communities and businesses adapt and recover quickly from disruptions.

Reviewing the National Infrastructure Protection Plan

Prior to starting the course, it will help you to learn more about the NIPP by either:

- Reviewing the NIPP and the Critical Infrastructure and Key Resources Support Annex to the National Response Framework (NRF).

    OR
- Completing the following Independent Study courses:
    - IS-860.c, National Infrastructure Protection Plan
    - IS-821.a, Critical Infrastructure and Key Resources Support Annex

Select this link to access a copy of the National Infrastructure Protection Plan document.

Select this link to access a copy of the Critical Infrastructure and Key Resources Support Annex document.

Sector Partnership Model

The NIPP relies on a sector partnership model as the primary national-level organizational structure for coordinating the Nation's critical infrastructure mission.

The national-level structure enables critical infrastructure public-private policy and planning coordination within and across 16 diverse sectors.

Sector Coordinating Councils

The sector partnership model encourages critical infrastructure owners and operators to create or identify Sector Coordinating Councils (SCCs) at the national level as the principal entity for coordinating with the government on a wide range of critical infrastructure security and resilience activities and issues.

The SCCs are self-organized, self-run, and self-governed, with a spokesperson designated by the sector membership. Specific membership will vary from sector to sector, reflecting the unique composition of each sector; however, membership should be representative of a broad base of owners, operators, associations, and other entities—both large and small—within a sector.

The SCCs enable owners and operators to interact on a wide range of sector-specific strategies, policies, activities, and issues. The SCCs serve as principal sector policy coordination and planning entities.

Government Coordinating Councils

The Government Coordinating Councils (GCCs) are the government counterparts for the corresponding SCCs and are formed to enable interagency and cross-jurisdictional coordination.

The GCCs include representatives from across various levels of government (Federal, State, local, or tribal), as appropriate to the operating landscape of each individual sector.

Each GCC is co-chaired by the U.S. Department of Homeland Security's Assistant Secretary for Infrastructure Protection or designee.

The GCCs are responsible for ensuring appropriate representation on the State, Local, Tribal, and Territorial Government Coordinating Council, and providing cross-sector coordination with State, local, and tribal governments. The GCC coordinates strategies, activities, policy, and communications across governmental entities within each sector.

Critical Infrastructure Cross-Sector Council

Cross-sector issues and interdependencies are addressed among the SCCs through the Critical Infrastructure Cross-Sector Council, which comprises the leadership of each of the SCCs.

The partnership coordinates cross-sector initiatives to support critical infrastructure security and resilience by identifying legislative issues that affect such initiatives and by raising awareness of issues in critical infrastructure security and resilience.

State, Local, Tribal, and Territorial Government Coordinating Council

The State, Local, Tribal, and Territorial Government Coordinating Council (SLTTGCC):

- Serves as a forum to ensure that State, local, tribal, and territorial homeland security partners are fully integrated as active participants in national critical infrastructure security efforts.
- Provides an organizational structure to coordinate across jurisdictions on State and local government-level critical infrastructure security and resilience guidance, strategies, and programs.
- Provides the State, local, tribal, or territorial perspective or feedback on a wide variety of critical infrastructure issues.

Regional Consortium Coordinating Council

The Regional Consortium Coordinating Council (RC3) brings together representatives of regional partnerships, groupings, and governance bodies to enable critical infrastructure security and resilience coordination among partners within and across geographical areas and sectors.

Critical Infrastructure Sectors

Currently there are 16 critical infrastructure sectors.

An overview of each of the critical infrastructure sectors and the Sector-Specific Agency (SSA) that is responsible for coordinating NIPP implementation within the sector are provided below.

Sector and Sector-Specific Agency	Overview
Chemical **Sector-Specific Agency:** Department of Homeland Security, Office of Infrastructure Protection	Several hundred thousand facilities in the United States in some manner use, manufacture, store, transport, or deliver chemicals, encompassing everything from petrochemical plants to pharmaceutical manufacturers. The Chemical Sector can be divided into five main segments, based on the end product produced: - Basic chemicals. - Specialty chemicals. - Agricultural chemicals. - Pharmaceuticals. - Consumer products.
Commercial Facilities **Sector-Specific Agency:** Department of Homeland Security, Office of Infrastructure Protection	The Commercial Facilities Sector includes a wide range of business, commercial, residential, and recreational facilities where large numbers of people congregate. Commercial facilities allow the general public to move freely without the deterrent of highly visible security barriers. This sector is diverse in both scope and function, and is divided into eight subsectors: Entertainment and Media, Gaming, Lodging, Outdoor Events, Public Assembly, Real Estate, Retail, and Sports Leagues.
Communications **Sector-Specific Agency:**	The Communications Sector is an integral component of the U.S. economy, as it underlies the operations of all businesses, public safety organizations, and government. Over the last 25 years, the Communications Sector has evolved from a predominantly voice-centric monolithic service into a diverse, competitive, and interconnected industry using global, satellite, and wireless transmission systems. Long-established processes and procedures for network security and rapid response and recovery under all hazards ensure the continued operation of vital communications

Department of Homeland Security, Office of Cybersecurity and Communications	services. Focused risk management and infrastructure protection are integral to the sector's business continuity planning and network design processes.

Critical Manufacturing
 	
Sector-Specific Agency:
 	
Department of Homeland Security, Office of Infrastructure Protection
	The Critical Manufacturing Sector is the newest addition to the critical infrastructure sectors identified in the NIPP. The Critical Manufacturing Sector is composed of four broad manufacturing industries, which were not represented in the original critical infrastructure sectors. These industries are:
	
	- Primary metal manufacturing:
	  - Iron and steel mills and ferro alloy manufacturing.
	  - Alumina and aluminum production and processing.
	  - Nonferrous metal (except aluminum) production and processing.
	- Machinery manufacturing: engine, turbine, and power transmission equipment manufacturing.
	- Electrical equipment, appliance, and component manufacturing.
	- Transportation equipment manufacturing:
	  - Motor vehicle manufacturing.
	  - Aerospace product and parts manufacturing.
	  - Railroad rolling stock manufacturing.
	  - Other transportation equipment manufacturing.

Dams **Sector-Specific Agency:** Department of Homeland Security, Office of Infrastructure Protection	The Dams Sector comprises the assets, systems, networks, and functions related to dam projects, navigation locks, levees, hurricane barriers, mine tailings and other industrial waste impoundments, and other similar water retention and/or control facilities. The Dams Sector is a vital and beneficial part of the Nation's infrastructure and continuously provides a wide range of economic, environmental, and social benefits, including: hydroelectric power, river navigation, water supply, wildlife habitat, waste management, flood control, and recreation.

 **Defense Industrial Base** **Sector-Specific Agency:** Department of Defense[1]	The Defense Industrial Base (DIB) Sector includes hundreds of thousands of domestic and foreign entities and subcontractors that perform work for the Department of Defense (DOD) and other Federal departments and agencies. These entities research, develop, design, produce, deliver, and maintain military weapons systems, subsystems, components, or parts. Defense-related products and services provided by the DIB Sector equip, inform, mobilize, deploy, and sustain forces conducting military operations worldwide. The size and diversity of the sector results in an extraordinarily large and complex collection of industrial sites and operators across 15 subsectors and more than 90 segments governed by multiple regulations, laws, treaties, and precedents.
 **Emergency Services** **Sector-Specific Agency:** Department of Homeland Security, Office of Infrastructure Protection	The Emergency Services Sector comprises the assets, systems, networks, and functions that are critical to maintain, protect, and preserve our safety and health in case of a natural or manmade disaster or terrorist incident. By protecting these elements, the sector is better able to support all critical infrastructure, essential governmental missions, and public services. These functions are vital to our Nation's security, public health and safety, economic vitality, and way of life. Through public and private-sector partnerships, this sector's mission is to accomplish the following: - Save lives; - Protect property and the environment; - Assist communities impacted by disasters (natural or manmade); and - Aid recovery from emergency situations.
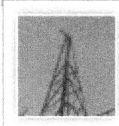 **Energy**	The Energy Sector consists of thousands of geographically dispersed electricity, oil, and natural gas assets that are connected by systems and networks. Without a stable energy supply, health and welfare is threatened and the economy of the United States cannot function. The energy infrastructure is divided into three interrelated segments: Electricity, Petroleum, and Natural Gas.

Sector-Specific Agency: Department of Energy	
Financial Services **Sector-Specific Agency:** Department of the Treasury	The Financial Services Sector is the backbone for the world economy, overseeing: • Deposit, consumer credit, and payment systems. • Credit and liquidity products. • Investment products. • Risk-transfer products (including insurance). As direct attacks and public statements by terrorist organizations demonstrate, the sector is a high-value and symbolic target. Additionally, large-scale power outages, recent natural disasters, and economic troubles demonstrate the wide range of potential threats facing the sector. Faced with these threats, financial regulators and private-sector owners and operators work collaboratively to maintain a high degree of resilience.
Food and Agriculture **Sector-Specific Agencies:** Department of Agriculture[2], Department of Health and Human Services[3]	The Food and Agriculture Sector is vast, comprising the Nation's agricultural production and food systems from farm to table. Because of the open nature of many portions of the Food and Agriculture Sector, attacks against the Nation using food or agricultural infrastructure or resources as a means to deliver biological, chemical, or radiological agents could have a devastating impact on public health and the economy.
Government Facilities	The Government Facilities Sector includes facilities owned or leased by all levels of government domestically or overseas. Many of these facilities are open to the public, such as courthouses, educational facilities, libraries, and archives. Other facilities not open to the public contain highly sensitive information, materials, processes, and equipment, such as military installations, embassies, and research facilities. These facilities are differentiated from

Sector-Specific Agencies: Department of Homeland Security and General Services Administration	other critical infrastructure sectors because they are uniquely governmental. The sector also includes the Education Facilities Subsector, which covers prekindergarten through 12th grade (pre-K through 12) schools, institutions of higher education, and business and trade schools. This subsector includes both government-owned facilities and facilities owned by private-sector entities, so it faces some unique challenges. The National Monuments and Icons Subsector encompasses a diverse array of assets, networks, systems, and functions located throughout the United States. Many National Monuments and Icons assets are listed in either the National Register of Historic Places or the List of National Historic Landmarks.
Healthcare and Public Health **Sector-Specific Agency:** Department of Health and Human Services	The systems, networks, services, facilities, functions, and roles needed to prevent disease and disability, treat patients, foster public health, and respond to public health emergencies span all levels of government and the private sector, and touch every citizen of the United States. Ensuring a resilient healthcare and public health system capable of withstanding disruption and poised to protect lives and health during emergencies is vital for the Nation's safety and security.
Information Technology **Sector-Specific Agency:**	The Information Technology (IT) Sector is central to our Nation's security, economy, public health, and safety. IT systems enable the Nation's economic activity, which is essential to maintaining homeland and national security. Many other critical infrastructure sectors rely on the IT Sector for products and services, including the reliable operation of networks and systems, and the movement and storage of critical data.

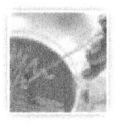

Department of Homeland Security, Office of Cybersecurity and Communications	
Nuclear Reactors, Materials, and Waste **Sector-Specific Agency:** Department of Homeland Security, Office of Infrastructure Protection	The Nuclear Reactors, Materials, and Waste Sector (or Nuclear Sector) owns, oversees, and operates commercial nuclear power reactors that provide power to millions of homes and businesses across the country. The sector also includes: - Nonpower nuclear reactors used for research, training, and radioisotope production. - Nuclear and radiological materials used in medical, industrial, and academic settings. - Nuclear fuel-cycle facilities. - The transportation, storage, and disposal of nuclear and radioactive materials and waste. The Nuclear Sector is composed of the following primary subsectors: Nuclear Facilities, Nuclear Materials, and Nuclear Waste. Nuclear critical infrastructure partners continue to build upon the sector's already high state of preparedness against all hazards, including acts of terrorism.
Transportation **Sector-Specific Agency:** Department of Homeland Security and Department of Transportation	The Transportation Systems Sector is a vast, open network of interdependent systems that moves millions of passengers and millions of tons of goods annually. What is unique about the Transportation Systems Sector is its part in the global transportation network. The Transportation Systems Sector relies on global partners to share critical information that can lead to more informed decisions by identifying and understanding threats, vulnerabilities, and consequences using global threat information and assessments. The sector is divided into six modes of transportation: Aviation, Maritime, Mass Transit, Highway, Freight Rail, and Pipeline.
	Safe drinking water and properly treated wastewater are critical to modern life. The former is a prerequisite for all human activity—physical, economic, and cultural. Wastewater treatment is important for preventing disease

Water and Wastewater Systems **Sector-Specific Agency:** Environmental Protection Agency	and protecting the environment. Therefore, from the standpoints of public health and economic impact, it is critical that we protect the Nation's drinking water and wastewater infrastructures, collectively known as the Water and Wastewater Systems Sector. There are approximately 160,000 public drinking water systems and more than 16,000 wastewater systems across the United States. More than 84 percent of the U.S. population receives its potable water from these drinking water systems, and more than 75 percent of the U.S. population has its sanitary sewage treated by these wastewater systems. The Water and Wastewater Systems Sector is a partnership of public and private drinking water and wastewater utilities; national and State associations; State, local, and tribal governments; research foundations; and Federal agencies that together have been ensuring the security and resilience of water services for decades. Water and Wastewater Systems Sector partners collaborate to be better prepared to prevent, detect, respond to, and recover from terrorist attacks and other intentional acts, natural disasters, and other hazards (i.e., the "all-hazards" approach).

Sector-Specific Plans and NIPP 2013 Supplements

Each critical infrastructure sector is responsible for developing and implementing a sector-specific plan (SSP), which details the application of the NIPP concepts to the unique characteristics and conditions of their sector. Sector-Specific Plans are being updated to align with the NIPP 2013.

NIPP 2013 supplements also serve as tools and resources that can be used by members of the critical infrastructure community as they implement specific aspects of the Plan.

- Connecting to the NICC and the NCCIC
- Executing a Critical Infrastructure Risk Management Approach
- Incorporating Resilience into Critical Infrastructure Projects
- National Protection and Programs Directorate Resources to Support Vulnerability Assessments

Critical Infrastructure Security and Resilience Partnerships

As outlined in the NIPP and Sector-Specific Plans, our ability to protect and improve resilience of the Nation's critical infrastructure depends largely on effective partnerships with the owners and operators of that infrastructure, as well as other partners who can inform and assist our efforts.

Security and resilience efforts are most efficient and effective when there is full participation of all governmental, nongovernmental, and private-sector partners.

Federal Government Roles and Responsibilities

The NIPP describes the following critical infrastructure security and resilience roles and responsibilities for the Federal Government:

- Identify, prioritize, and coordinate Federal action in support of the protection of critical infrastructure.
- Integrate critical infrastructure protective programs with the Nation's all-hazards approach to domestic incident management.
- Integrate national efforts for the security and resilience of critical infrastructure.
- Document and share lessons learned.

Owner and Operator Roles and Responsibilities

Owners and operators of critical infrastructure are ultimately responsible for its security and resilience. Their responsibilities may be described using the following categories:

Planning

- Developing an awareness of critical dependencies and interdependencies at the sector, enterprise, and facility levels.
- Developing and coordinating protective and emergency response actions, plans, and programs with appropriate Federal, State, local, tribal, and territorial government authorities.
- Establishing continuity plans and programs that facilitate the performance of critical functions during an emergency or until normal operations can be resumed.

Forming Partnerships

- Participating in the NIPP sector partnership model (including Sector Coordinating Councils).
- Participating in Federal, State, local, tribal, and territorial government critical infrastructure security and resilience and emergency management programs and coordinating structures.
- Entering into operational mutual aid agreements with other industry partners.
- Working to identify and reduce barriers to public-private partnerships.

Sharing Information

- Participating in NIPP sector partnership model information-sharing mechanisms.
- Assisting and supporting Federal, State, local, tribal, and territorial government critical infrastructure data collection and protection efforts.
- Providing technical expertise to the Sector-Specific Agencies and Department of Homeland Security.
- Identifying and communicating requirements to the Department of Homeland Security and/or the Sector-Specific Agencies and State and local governments for critical infrastructure security and resilience-related research and development.
- Sharing security-related best practices with other industry partners.

Managing Risk

- Performing comprehensive risk assessments tailored to the specific sector, enterprise, or facility risk landscape.
- Implementing protective actions and programs to reduce identified vulnerabilities appropriate to the level of risk presented.
- Establishing cybersecurity programs within the organization.
- Adhering to recognized industry best business practices and standards, including those with a cybersecurity nexus.
- Establishing resilient, robust, and/or redundant operational systems or capabilities associated with critical functions.
- Adopting and implementing effective workforce security assurance programs to mitigate potential insider threats.

Ensuring Continuous Improvement

- Promoting critical infrastructure security and resilience education, training, and awareness programs.
- Participating in regular critical infrastructure security and resilience-focused training and exercise programs with other public- and private-sector partners.

State, Local, Tribal, and Territorial (SLTT) Government Responsibilities

Key critical infrastructure security and resilience responsibilities at the SLTT level also include:

- Planning.
- Forming partnerships.
- Sharing information.
- Managing risk.
- Ensuring continuous improvement.

While the major headings describing the responsibilities are the same, the specific responsibilities of owners and operators and of jurisdictions differ in the details.

Critical Infrastructure Security and Resilience Activities Checklists

Planning Activities

☐ Develop a consistent approach to critical infrastructure identification.

- ☐ Identify critical infrastructure assets and systems.
- ☐ Identify dependencies, interdependencies, and key nodes within the jurisdiction.

☐ Obtain copies of existing hazard mitigation and emergency operations plans, including:

- ☐ Critical infrastructure security and resilience plans.
- ☐ Hazard mitigation plans (also called hazard plans or mitigation plans).
- ☐ Emergency operations plans/Emergency response plans.
- ☐ Continuity of operations plans.

☐ Either:

- ☐ Review, collaborate as necessary, and update existing plans to ensure that they address critical infrastructure security and resilience; OR
- ☐ Develop a unique critical infrastructure security and resilience plan and program for the area of responsibility.

☐ Ensure that plans identify:

- ☐ Critical infrastructure security and resilience:

- ○ ☐ Roles and responsibilities.
- ○ ☐ Partners within the jurisdiction.
- ○ ☐ Information-sharing mechanisms (both for receiving and for reporting information).
  - ☐ How critical infrastructure information is used and, if necessary, how it is protected.
  - ☐ The process used to manage risk to critical infrastructure.
  - ☐ How the jurisdiction will leverage ongoing emergency preparedness and mitigation activities for critical infrastructure security and resilience.

☐ Critical infrastructure or other plans also may identify:

- ☐ Whether gaps exist between the jurisdiction's current approach and those roles and responsibilities outlined in the NIPP or in an SSP, and how the gaps will be addressed.
- ☐ Whether any roles and responsibilities should be revised, modified, or consolidated to accommodate the unique operating attributes of the jurisdiction.
- ☐ How the jurisdiction will maintain operational awareness of the performance of the critical infrastructure security and resilience roles assigned to different offices, agencies, or localities.
- ☐ How the jurisdiction will coordinate its critical infrastructure security and resilience roles and responsibilities with other jurisdictions and the Federal Government.
- ☐ Unique geographical issues, including transborder concerns.

Partnership Activities

☐ Identify potential critical infrastructure security and resilience partners by leveraging existing public-private partnerships designed to enhance emergency management and community protection and recovery functions. Examples include:

- ☐ Business alliances and partnerships.
- ☐ Citizen Corps.
- ☐ State and regional partnerships.

☐ As appropriate, participate in critical infrastructure sector partnership councils and other forums, including:

- ☐ Sector-specific GCCs and SCCs.

- ☐ The State, Local, Tribal, and Territorial Government Coordinating Council (SLTTGCC).
- ☐ Other critical infrastructure governance and planning efforts relevant to the given jurisdiction.

☐ Identify other potential partners and partnership entities:

- ☐ Critical infrastructure owners and operators.
- ☐ Government partners:
  - ☐ DHS and other Federal departments, agencies, and offices.
  - ☐ State, local, tribal, and territorial governments.
- ☐ Critical infrastructure sector partnership councils and other forums (see below).
- ☐ Professional associations.
- ☐ Advisory councils.
- ☐ Academia and research centers.
- ☐ Nongovernmental organizations.
- ☐ Others.

☐ Invite potential partners to participate.

- ☐ Present the value proposition as necessary.
- ☐ Resolve partnership challenges as necessary.
- ☐ Identify how and when partners will meet and/or exchange information.
- ☐ Establish ground rules for information exchange. For example, identify what information can be shared outside the partnership and what cannot be shared.

☐ Establish critical infrastructure partnership goals. Identify specific security and resilience goals that are not currently met under existing hazard mitigation, emergency management, or other programs.

☐ As necessary, coordinate protective activities, preparedness programs, and resource support among local jurisdictions, regional organizations, and private-sector partners.

Information-Sharing Activities

☐ Determine information needs to maintain situational awareness and protect critical infrastructure. Ask:

- ☐ What questions am I trying to answer (who, what, when, where, how)?
- ☐ Why do I need this information?
- ☐ What am I going to do with this information?

☐ Identify information assets (what you currently have or collect) and determine what you can through your own research.

☐ Identify other information sources to meet needs.

☐ Facilitate the sharing of real-time threat and incident information through partnerships and information-sharing mechanisms.

☐ Establish mechanisms for collecting information from critical infrastructure employees and others, identifying:

- ☐ How to encourage participation.
- ☐ How to capture reported information.
- ☐ How to validate reported information (see below).
- ☐ How to forward information.

☐ Check collected information for reliability and validity/accuracy.

- ☐ Assess reliability of the source by asking:
    - ☐ Does the source have a history of reliability?
    - ☐ Are there any doubts about the source's competency?
    - ☐ Are there any doubts about the trustworthiness of the source?
    - ☐ Was the source in a position to accurately observe the information?
- ☐ Double-check the facts. Assess validity/accuracy of the information by asking:
    - ☐ Can the information be confirmed by other independent sources?
    - ☐ Is the information logical?
    - ☐ Is the information consistent with other information?
    - ☐ Are there contradictions in the information that need to be addressed?

☐ Share critical infrastructure information to enable prioritized security and restoration of critical public services, facilities, utilities, and functions within the jurisdiction.

Risk Management Activities

- ☐ Identify threats from adversaries, natural disasters, and technological hazards that could affect critical infrastructure.

    - ☐ Obtain threat assessment information concerning terrorism through Federal and other appropriate channels.
    - ☐ For natural disasters and accidental hazards, use best-available analytic tools and historical data to estimate the likelihood of these events.

- ☐ Assess vulnerabilities and consequences.

    - ☐ Assess critical infrastructure vulnerabilities to identified threats.
        - ☐ Leverage existing vulnerability assessment programs and tools.
        - ☐ Incorporate completed vulnerability assessment data.
    - ☐ Assess potential consequences to critical infrastructure based on identified threats and vulnerabilities.
    - ☐ Incorporate dependency, interdependency, and other analyses, as needed.

- ☐ Implement protective programs and measures.

    - ☐ Identify effective practices based on recognized industry best business practices and standards.
    - ☐ Leverage existing Federal and other programs. Coordinate with State, regional, and territorial representatives concerning Federal assistance and initiatives. For example:
        - ☐ Act as a conduit for requests for Federal assistance when the threat or current situation exceeds the capabilities of the jurisdiction and the private entities resident within it.
        - ☐ Provide information to owners and operators, as part of the grants process and/or homeland security strategy updates, regarding State priorities, requirements, and critical infrastructure funding needs.
    - ☐ Identify and communicate to DHS requirements from owners and operators for research and development related to critical infrastructure.
    - ☐ Develop a prioritized implementation plan.
        - ☐ Describe assigned tasks with deadlines.
        - ☐ Provide a means to chart progress in reaching milestones.
        - ☐ Incorporate implementation into existing plans as needed.
    - ☐ Implement programs and measures.
        - ☐ Establish continuity plans and programs that facilitate the performance of critical functions during an emergency or until normal operations can be resumed.

- ☐ Provide response and protective measures, as appropriate, where there are gaps and where local entities lack the resources needed to address those gaps.

Ensuring Continuous Improvement Activities

☐ Participate in education and training offered by government and sector partners as appropriate.

- ☐ Arrange for training to be conducted in your jurisdiction as possible.
- ☐ Encourage all stakeholders to participate in training sessions.

☐ Participate in industry-related and professional or trade association training as needed.

- ☐ Arrange for training to be conducted in your jurisdiction as possible.
- ☐ Encourage all stakeholders to participate in training sessions.

☐ Test and practice protective measures with all stakeholders.

- ☐ Conduct red-team testing.
- ☐ Practice procedures.

☐ Participate in exercises of critical infrastructure security and resilience programs and plans.

- ☐ Develop and conduct exercises.
- ☐ Include critical infrastructure security and resilience in existing exercises.
- ☐ Participate in State and regional exercises.

☐ Document lessons learned from predisaster mitigation efforts and testing, exercises, and actual incidents and apply that learning, where applicable, to the critical infrastructure context.

☐ Develop implementation plan and take corrective actions.

- ☐ Identify additional training needs.
- ☐ Identify other needed actions.

- ☐ Coordinate with other government and private-sector partners as needed to implement corrective actions.

☐ Add or update implementation and other plans as necessary.

- ☐ Critical infrastructure security and resilience plans.
- ☐ Hazard mitigation plans (also called hazard plans or mitigation plans).
- ☐ Emergency operations or response plans.
- ☐ Continuity of operations plans.

Critical Infrastructure Security and Resilience Activities

Critical infrastructure security and resilience activities have a significant amount of overlap between them. For example:

- Information-sharing takes place within a partnership framework and supports risk management processes.
- Managing risk may reveal a need to implement continuous improvement activities (e.g., testing and exercising) or to update plans.
- Critical infrastructure activities also may be conducted concurrently. For example, tabletop exercises can be used to develop partnerships and initiate planning.

Many Starting Points

The diagram of the critical infrastructure security and resilience activities is circular because there is no discrete beginning point to the process.

You may already have preexisting partnerships, information-sharing and risk management processes, and continuous improvement programs in place before the critical infrastructure security and resilience planning process begins.

Critical infrastructure partners should leverage existing programs and processes to the maximum extent possible.

Planning

The planning process identifies your critical infrastructure – what you need to protect within your area of responsibility.

During planning, ask yourself what you need to protect in order to accomplish your mission.

- Are you an official responsible for critical infrastructure security and resilience, whose overall mission is to protect the way of life for your community?
- Are you a critical infrastructure owner or operator, whose mission is to provide a vital service to your community, region or the Nation?

Planning Activities

Recommended planning activities for officials with critical infrastructure security and resilience responsibilities include:

- Developing a consistent approach to critical infrastructure identification.
- Identifying critical infrastructure assets and systems.
- Tracing critical infrastructure dependencies.
- Developing security and resilience plans or updating existing plans to include critical infrastructure security and resilience.

Critical Infrastructure Security and Resilience: Planning Activities

This checklist provides recommended critical infrastructure security and resilience planning activities for State, local, tribal, and territorial (SLTT) governments.

☐ Develop a consistent approach to critical infrastructure identification.

- ☐ Identify critical infrastructure assets and systems.
- ☐ Identify dependencies, interdependencies, and key nodes within the jurisdiction.

☐ Obtain copies of existing hazard mitigation and emergency operations plans, including:

- ☐ Critical infrastructure security and resilience plans.
- ☐ Hazard mitigation plans (also called hazard plans or mitigation plans).
- ☐ Emergency operations plans/Emergency response plans.

- ☐ Continuity of operations plans.

☐ Either:

- ☐ Review, collaborate as necessary, and update existing plans to ensure that they address critical infrastructure security and resilience; OR
- ☐ Develop a unique critical infrastructure security and resilience plan and program for the area of responsibility.

☐ Ensure that plans identify:

- ☐ Critical infrastructure security and resilience:
    - ☐ Roles and responsibilities.
    - ☐ Partners within the jurisdiction.
    - ☐ Information-sharing mechanisms (both for receiving and for reporting information).
- ☐ How critical infrastructure information is used and, if necessary, how it is protected.
- ☐ The process used to manage risk to critical infrastructure.
- ☐ How the jurisdiction will leverage ongoing emergency preparedness and mitigation activities for critical infrastructure security and resilience.

☐ Critical infrastructure or other plans also may identify:

- ☐ Whether gaps exist between the jurisdiction's current approach and those roles and responsibilities outlined in the NIPP or in an SSP, and how the gaps will be addressed.
- ☐ Whether any roles and responsibilities should be revised, modified, or consolidated to accommodate the unique operating attributes of the jurisdiction.
- ☐ How the jurisdiction will maintain operational awareness of the performance of the critical infrastructure security and resilience roles assigned to different offices, agencies, or localities.
- ☐ How the jurisdiction will coordinate its critical infrastructure security and resilience roles and responsibilities with other jurisdictions and the Federal Government.
- ☐ Unique geographical issues, including transborder concerns.

Developing a Consistent Approach

State, local, tribal, territorial, or regional points of contact may be able to provide relevant criteria and information to help develop a consistent approach to critical infrastructure identification.

The Portland/Vancouver Urban Area report described on the following screens provides a detailed explanation of the model that was used for identifying critical infrastructure.

Whatever the model used, it should be consistent with response and resilience planning.

Portland/Vancouver Urban Area Report

The Portland, Oregon and Vancouver, Washington urban areas in 2007 jointly produced the Critical Infrastructure Protection Plan: Portland/Vancouver Urban Area report.

This document describes the critical infrastructure protection planning process and is a guide for future development.

Select this link to access a copy of the Critical Infrastructure Protection Plan: Portland/Vancouver Urban Area document.

Critical Infrastructure Identification and Prioritization

As described in the Portland/Vancouver report, the development process yielded several positive results.

- First, a definition of critical infrastructure for the region was established.
- Next, a methodology for assessing criticality was developed and used to prioritize the critical infrastructure assets within the urban area.
- Finally, a follow-on workshop conducted with owners and operators in the region enhanced their understanding of the importance of dependencies to critical infrastructure security and resilience planning.

Identifying Critical Infrastructure

After establishing an approach for identifying and ranking critical infrastructure, the next step is to implement that process. Doing so helps to identify and prioritize the critical infrastructure in your area of responsibility.

It is important to include critical infrastructure owners and operators in this process.

Points of Failure and Dependencies

While identifying what needs to be protected, you also should determine whether there are specific points of failure that would compromise your mission.

For example:
A local dam generates power for your region using five of its six turbines; the sixth turbine is for backup use. The dam would continue to generate sufficient power if one turbine failed. Something that would impact all of the turbines at once – such as a crash of the computer operating system – is a potential point of failure and needs to be addressed in your planning.

Tracing Dependencies

The next step is to trace the dependencies among critical infrastructure. Participation by owners and operators is critical to tracing dependencies.

Owners and operators should answer questions such as:

- What do we need to remain resilient and to recover from a disaster? Do we need energy, fuel, communications, or transportation for key employees?
- If there are backup systems in place, what is needed to keep them in operation?

Developing or Updating Plans

There are several options for building critical infrastructure security and resilience plans. Officials responsible for critical infrastructure security and resilience should determine which of the following options to use:

- Review, collaborate as necessary, and update existing plans to ensure that they address critical infrastructure security and resilience; OR
- Develop a unique critical infrastructure security and resilience plan and program for the area of responsibility.

Existing Plans

You may have already accomplished the planning process. There may be existing critical infrastructure security and resilience, response, or continuity of operations plans within your area of responsibility.

These include:

- Critical infrastructure security and resilience plans.
- Hazard mitigation plans (also called hazard plans or mitigation plans).
- Emergency operations or response plans.
- Continuity of operations or business continuity plans.
- Risk management plans.

Planning Categories

If you have critical infrastructure responsibilities within your jurisdiction, you should review all relevant plans to determine whether they address your infrastructure security and resilience needs.

When reviewing or developing plans, you should ensure that they explicitly address six broad categories:

- Critical infrastructure security and resilience roles and responsibilities.
- Partnership building and information sharing.
- Risk management.
- Critical infrastructure data use and protection.
- Leveraging of ongoing emergency preparedness activities.
- Integration of Federal critical infrastructure security and resilience and recovery activities.

Critical Infrastructure Security and Resilience Plans

Critical infrastructure security and resilience plans also should address the following:

- Whether gaps exist between the jurisdiction's current approach and those roles and responsibilities outlined in the NIPP or in a Sector-Specific Plan, and how the gaps will be addressed.
- Whether any roles and responsibilities should be revised, modified, or consolidated to accommodate the unique operating attributes of the jurisdiction.
- How the jurisdiction will maintain operational awareness of the performance of the critical infrastructure security and resilience roles assigned to different offices, agencies, or localities.
- How the jurisdiction will coordinate its critical infrastructure security and resilience roles and responsibilities with other jurisdictions and the Federal Government.
- Unique geographical issues, including transborder concerns, dependencies, and interdependencies among the sectors within the jurisdiction.

Washington State Region 6

Region 6 (geographic King County) in Washington State produced a Critical Infrastructure Protection Plan in September 2005.

The plan's goal was to define the processes for ensuring that decisionmakers, owners and operators, and governmental entities have the information necessary to make judgments about protection.

Region 6 still is served well to this day by the plan's descriptions of: roles and responsibilities; information sharing and coordination; and decisionmaking processes.

Select this link to access a copy of the Washington State Region 6 plan.

Resources

Select the links below for additional information relating to the content of this lesson.

Information Sheets

- Critical Infrastructure Security and Resilience Activities Checklists
- Critical Infrastructure Sectors
- Owner and Operator Roles and Responsibilities
- Sector Partnership Model: Key Components

Publications

- Critical Infrastructure and Key Resources Support Annex
- National Infrastructure Protection Plan

Training Courses

- IS-821.a, National Response Framework Critical Infrastructure Support Annex
- IS-860.c, National Infrastructure Protection Plan
- IS-913.A: Critical Infrastructure Security and Resilience: Achieving Results through Partnership and Collaboration

Web Pages

- Critical Infrastructure Security Web site
- Critical Infrastructure Resources
- Critical Infrastructure Training
- Homeland Security Information Network (HSIN)
- Office of Infrastructure Protection (DHS) Web site
- National Infrastructure Protection Plan Web site

Lesson Summary

In this lesson, you learned about critical infrastructure security and resilience roles and responsibilities and planning activities.

In the next lesson, you will learn more about forming partnerships.

Lesson 2: Forming Partnerships

Lesson Overview

This lesson describes the importance of forming partnerships and engaging stakeholders to protect critical infrastructure assets and facilities.

Upon completing this lesson, you should be able to:

- List the advantages of forming critical infrastructure partnerships.
- Describe critical infrastructure security and resilience partnership activities.
- Identify potential critical infrastructure partners.

Infrastructure Protection

Todd Keil, Assistant Secretary, Office of Infrastructure Protection
Public private partnerships are so important because nobody can do this alone. DHS can't do it alone. The Federal Government can't do it alone. The State governments, the sports leagues - can't do it themselves. But when you put all of us together, it's an amazing force for change and it's an amazing force that increases the security of our country.

Michael Rodriguez, Director of Security, U.S. Open
If you don't have that connection between the private sector and the Federal Government, the Federal Government will not know what they can do to support us, and what they can give us as far as training and support in those areas.

Charles Burns, Security Director, Indy Racing League
We in the private sports entity rely on the public sector for intelligence, techniques, and equipment to make sure that our venues are safe for all the spectators and personnel that are working there.

Gerry Cavis, Managing Director, NASCAR Security
Without information sharing there is just no way we can see what's coming at us without talking to one another. Homeland Security has provided a venue for that - for us to meet and to share information every chance that we get. And to constantly be an update source for us.

Michael Rodriguez
As we learned post 9-11, vigilance is the most important thing that we do in the security world and it's how to continue to prepare yourself from a security aspect on protecting patrons.

Todd Keil
You have to have robust policies and procedures in place. You have to practice and exercise those policies and procedures. So be it a manmade incident or a natural disaster, it comes down to all hazards, and it comes down to being prepared, and practicing and exercising and being able to respond.

Gerry Cavis
It's very, very important that we make a plan and then we test it to see if it's going to work prior to the event.

Charles Burns
If something happens and you haven't trained, then we have a major problem.

Turner Madden, Co-Chair, Commercial Facilities Sector Coordinating Council
Even though we in the private sector are required to secure our own facilities, with us working together as partners, we can better protect the private sector and the country.

Gerry Cavis
If we don't protect our public spaces, then we've lost to terrorism. It's not good enough to have assets in place for the investigative, after the fact, after the incident. We want to stop it from happening. By putting everybody together, that gives us an opportunity to be proactive and preventative in nature.

Todd Keil
If you have a plan, that's great, but if people don't exercise it they really don't know what they're going to do in the event something happens. In the event of an incident, there are a lot of things that happen really fast that might be very shocking, and if you don't practice something, that doesn't happen naturally during an incident. So practicing and exercising is the most important element in any type of security plan.

UPDATE: The following officials have left the noted positions since the making of this video:

- Todd Keil, Former Assistant Secretary, Office of Infrastructure Protection
- Charles Burns, Former Security Director, Indy Racing League
- Gerry Cavis, Former Managing Director, NASCAR Security
- Turner Madden, Former Co-Chair, Commercial Facilities Sector Coordinating Council

Forming Partnerships

The second critical infrastructure security and resilience activity is forming partnerships.

Members of the State, Local, Tribal, and Territorial Government Coordinating Council (SLTTGCC) and other State and local officials have indicated that making infrastructure more resilient depends on the strength of a jurisdiction's relationship with owners and operators in its region.

Engaging Owners and Operators

Governments at all levels have established a variety of mechanisms to reach out to and engage the private sector in emergency response planning, including private-sector advisory councils and regional critical infrastructure forums.

Because owners and operators are responsible for the resilience of their own critical infrastructure, government's role as part of this engagement must include encouraging and providing incentives to owners and operators to take action.

Factors Critical to Effective Partnerships

Based on a U.S. Government Accountability Office study, the following factors are considered essential to establishing effective relationships and addressing partnership challenges:

- Fostering trust and respect.
- Establishing effective, timely, and appropriately secure communication.
- Generating clearly identifiable membership benefits.

Value Proposition of Public-Private Partnerships

Public-private partnerships provide the foundation for critical infrastructure security and resilience.

The principal value of these partnerships for owners and operators is the receipt of timely, accurate, and useful threat/hazard information. This information sharing:

- Facilitates more informed decisionmaking on how best to protect critical infrastructure.
- Provides business justification for investing in protective measures.

Value Proposition: Additional Benefits

Benefits of critical infrastructure security and resilience partnerships for owners and operators also include:

- Stakeholder input into policies and procedures that generate supportable, successful solutions.
- Voluntary adoption of widely accepted protective measures and practices.
- Identification and formulation of potential solutions to common critical infrastructure security and resilience challenges.
- Collaborative research and development initiatives to enhance future security and resilience efforts.
- Expanded availability of resources and technical assistance to support business continuity planning.
- Development of interdependency studies, exercises, symposiums, training sessions, and computer modeling.
- Enhanced time-sensitive information sharing both during steady-state and incident-related activities.
- Improved processes to facilitate rapid recovery for critical infrastructure facilities and services.

Partnership Activities

Recommended partnership activities for officials with critical infrastructure responsibilities include:

- Identifying existing and potential partners (individuals and organizations).
- Inviting partners to participate. This includes addressing the benefits of and challenges to partnerships.
- Establishing partnership goals.
- Coordinating security and recovery activities, preparedness programs, and resource support among local jurisdictions, regional organizations, and private-sector partners.

This checklist provides recommended critical infrastructure security and resilience partnership activities for State, local, tribal, and territorial (SLTT) governments.

- ☐ Identify potential critical infrastructure security and resilience partners by leveraging existing public-private partnerships that are designed to enhance emergency management, protection, and recovery functions. Examples include:

    - ☐ Business alliances and partnerships.
    - ☐ Citizen Corps.

- ☐ State and regional partnerships.

☐ As appropriate, participate in critical infrastructure sector partnership councils and other forums, including:

- ☐ Sector-specific GCCs and SCCs.
- ☐ The State, Local, Tribal, and Territorial Government Coordinating Council (SLTTGCC).
- ☐ Other critical infrastructure governance and planning efforts relevant to the given jurisdiction.

☐ Identify other potential partners and partnership entities:

- ☐ Critical infrastructure owners and operators.
- ☐ Government partners:
    - ☐ DHS and other Federal departments, agencies, and offices.
    - ☐ State, local, tribal, and territorial governments.
- ☐ Critical infrastructure sector partnership councils and other forums (see below).
- ☐ Professional associations.
- ☐ Advisory councils.
- ☐ Academia and research centers.
- ☐ Nongovernmental organizations.
- ☐ Others.

☐ Invite potential partners to participate.

- ☐ Present the value proposition as necessary.
- ☐ Resolve partnership challenges as necessary.
- ☐ Identify how and when partners will meet and/or exchange information.
- ☐ Establish ground rules for information exchange. For example, identify what information can be shared outside the partnership and what cannot be shared.

☐ Establish critical infrastructure partnership goals.
Identify specific security and resilience goals that are not currently met under existing hazard mitigation, emergency management, or other programs.

☐ As necessary, coordinate protective activities, preparedness programs, and resource support among local jurisdictions, regional organizations, and private-sector partners.

Identifying Critical Infrastructure Partners

Public and private-sector organizations can help bolster the Nation's preparedness by participating in partnerships to identify common concerns and needs, share information, share successful models and effective practices, train and exercise together, and form more partnerships across the country.

Forming partnerships for critical infrastructure security and resilience involves:

- Leveraging existing public-private partnerships.
- Identifying and contacting potential partners and partnership entities.

Existing Partnerships

Many partnerships exist that form a basis for critical infrastructure security and resilience. Security, resilience, and recovery plans are sources for identifying existing partnerships.

For example, many jurisdictions actively engage public-private partners to improve capabilities for emergency management.

National

- **Business Emergency Operations Center (BEOC) Alliance:** The BEOC Alliance functions as a private-sector advocate in emergency management functions (preparedness, prevention/mitigation, response, recovery). Services include but are not limited to periodic symposia and threat briefings, information sharing, exercise design to include modeling and simulation, business continuity, critical infrastructure interdependencies, and collaborations (strategic, tactical, and operational). The founding entity of the BEOC Alliance is the New Jersey Business Force, which is a business unit under the Alliance.
- **Business Executives for National Security (BENS):** BENS, a nationwide, nonpartisan organization, is a channel through which senior business executives can help enhance the Nation's security. BENS members use their business experience to help government leaders implement solutions to the most challenging national security problems. BENS is expanding these public-private partnerships into all aspects of homeland security—helping to guard against cyber attack, tracking terrorists' financial assets, securing the Nation's ports, and preparing State and local governments to deal with catastrophic events or terrorist attacks.
- **Citizen Corps:** Citizen Corps is the grassroots movement to strengthen community safety and preparedness through increased civic engagement.

Citizen Corps is administered by the Federal Emergency Management Agency, but implemented locally. Communities across the country have created Citizen Corps Councils as effective public-private partnerships to make their communities safer, more prepared, and more resilient when incidents occur.

Regional

- **All Hazards Consortium (AHC):** The AHC is a multi-State, multi-urban area nonprofit formed to create new resources and partnerships for member States (NC, DC, MD, VA, WV, DE, PA, NJ, and NY) to support regional multi-State collaboration efforts among all stakeholders from government, private sector, higher education, and nonprofit/volunteer organizations. It focuses on three key areas: catastrophic planning, fusion/information sharing, and private-sector integration into critical infrastructure security efforts.
- **ChicagoFIRST:** ChicagoFIRST is a nonprofit association of private-sector critical infrastructure firms in the Chicago area that collaborate with one another and with government at all levels on homeland security and emergency management issues in order to promote the resilience of its members and the Chicago business community.
- **Dallas/Fort Worth First (DFW First):** DFW First is a regional coalition created to support homeland security critical infrastructure partnership initiatives involving the financial services and banking sector. The DFW First "Beyond the 4 Walls" campaign is designed to align a financial institution's business continuity and emergency preparation processes with outside agencies responsible for first response activities.
- **Pacific Northwest Economic Region (PNWER):** The PNWER is a regional organization created by the States of Alaska, Idaho, Oregon, Montana, and Washington and the Canadian provinces and territories of British Columbia, Alberta, Saskatchewan, Northwest Territories, and the Yukon. PNWER, through its Pacific Northwest Center for Regional Disaster Resilience, works with key public and private stakeholders to create and implement workable solutions to local and regional infrastructure vulnerability and other related needs. PNWER accomplishes this by raising awareness of infrastructure interdependencies, providing training and education, and developing tools, technologies, and approaches that build on existing capabilities and can be utilized across the United States, Canada, and the international community.

State

- **Arizona:** The State of Arizona's Division of Emergency Management (ADEM) has incorporated business, corporations, and enterprises that have a stake in protecting critical infrastructure into the State Emergency

Response and Recovery Plan. The private-sector entities that meet the criteria of critical infrastructure sectors and their associates are encouraged to join Arizona's efforts in the mitigation, preparedness, response and recovery of incidents and events. ADEM directs situational awareness information to its critical information partners via an electronically distributed information bulletin.

- **Missouri:** The Missouri Public Private Partnership (MOP3) Committee is a voluntary coalition of Missouri's private- and public-sector leaders, who share a commitment to strengthening the capacity of the State to prevent, prepare for, respond to, and recover from disasters. MOP3 partners work to reduce the impact of emergencies on their communities by pledging resources and offering support services. The committee promotes the application of best business practices; partnering on planning, training, and exercise development; fostering participation in intelligence/information fusion; and providing a private-sector platform to address issues and concerns for homeland security initiatives.
- **Utah:** At the forefront of Utah's public-private partnership is the Private Sector Homeland Security Coordinating Council. Membership includes representatives from the private sector, nongovernment organizations, and local/State/Federal government. Be Ready Utah's "Ready Your Business" focuses on preparing businesses for potential emergencies and disasters. This preparation includes the most essential elements, including a 12-step program for basic business continuity planning.

Tribal Nation

- **Indian Health Program:** Emergency preparedness in California is unique in that over 170 indigenous tribes (representing about 20% of the 500 tribal groups in the United States) are represented by the 627,562 American Indians throughout the State. The California Area Office of the Indian Health Service (IHS), the California Indian Health Program (IHP), and the California Emergency Preparedness Office, in collaboration with the Native American Alliance for Emergency Preparedness (NAAEP) is creating capacity among its healthcare providers across California's Indian Country to respond appropriately to natural and manmade threats and health emergencies.

Major Urban Areas

- **Dallas, TX:** The Dallas Emergency Response Team (DERT) is a public-private partnership for collaboration and communication between local government and the business community. The DERT partnership focuses on communications before, during, and after emergencies, exercising disaster plans, and sharing training opportunities for anyone seeking to become better informed and better prepared.

- **New York, NY:** The Public/Private Initiatives Unit at the New York City Office of Emergency Management (OEM) is dedicated to partnering with the private sector to increase the resilience of the city's business community and to ensure that private organizations have all the information they need before, during, and after an emergency. OEM's Public/Private Initiatives Unit is dedicated specifically to managing and improving the agency's relationships with and programs for private-sector organizations in New York City.
- **San Diego, CA:** The ReadySanDiego Business Alliance (BA) is a coalition of businesses that can contribute resources, participate in preparedness activities, and assist in disaster response and recovery activities. The BA addresses issues specific to business needs with support from the Office of Emergency Services. The BA incorporates private and nonprofit sectors in its planning processes.

County

- **Fairfax County, VA:** Fairfax County's Office of Emergency Management has developed a partnership with several organizations to develop a Pre-Disaster Recovery Plan. Partners include local nonprofits, businesses, boards, authorities, commissions, jurisdictional neighbors, and regional, State, and Federal partners. The purpose of the Pre-Disaster Recovery Plan is to provide Fairfax County with a single reference for guiding policy and action during recovery from a significant natural or human-caused disaster.
- **Santa Rosa County, FL:** SAFER Santa Rosa County is a humanitarian association of independent organizations that may be active in all phases of disaster. Its mission is to foster efficient, streamlined service delivery to people affected by disasters, while eliminating unnecessary duplication of effort, through cooperation in the four phases of disaster: preparation, response, recovery, and mitigation.

Identifying Potential Critical Infrastructure Partners

Potential partners include:

- Critical infrastructure owners and operators.
- Government organizations (State, local, tribal, territorial, regional, and Federal entities).
- Critical infrastructure sector councils, associations, and other organizations.
- Professional, trade, and business associations.
- Advisory councils.
- Academia and research centers.
- Nongovernmental organizations.

Inviting Partners

It is important to understand and demonstrate the value proposition of participating in critical infrastructure security and resilience partnerships when inviting potential partners to the table. The value proposition was covered earlier in this lesson.

At the same time, it may be necessary to resolve challenges involved in forming partnerships, such as concerns about information sharing. Several challenges and approaches for resolving them are identified on the following screens.

Sharing Sensitive or Proprietary Information

Owners and operators often express concerns about sharing trade information that is sensitive or proprietary.

Information-sharing concerns are alleviated by trust, which is built only over time. Leveraging existing partnerships can help to build trust. Owner and operator concerns also can be allayed by developing agreements in advance about the use of shared information.

Programs such as the Federal Protected Critical Infrastructure Information (PCII) Program help to ensure that sensitive and proprietary information is protected from disclosure.

Protected Critical Infrastructure Information Program

The Protected Critical Infrastructure Information (PCII) Program is a Federal information-protection program that enhances information sharing between the private sector and the government. PCII information can be accessed only in accordance with strict safeguarding and handling requirements.

The Department of Homeland Security and other Federal, State, and local analysts use PCII to:

- Analyze and secure critical infrastructure and protected systems,
- Identify vulnerabilities and develop risk assessments, and
- Enhance recovery preparedness measures.

An important aspect of the program is that protected critical infrastructure information, once validated, cannot be used for regulatory purposes. This is a concern of all industries.

PCII also is protected from:

- Freedom of Information Act (FOIA) disclosure,
- State and local disclosure laws, and
- Use in civil litigation.

Select this link for additional information about PCII.

Lack of Imminent Threat

The difficulty in establishing a viable business case for building preparedness capabilities when there is no recent incident or clearly identified imminent threat or hazard is a challenge in some sectors.

Engagement in partnerships and the sharing of effective practices and threat/hazard information will help to establish the case for security and resilience efforts. For example, the American Hotel & Lodging Association has teamed up with DHS to encourage and educate lodging employees to recognize, report, and react to suspicious and crisis situations.

Differing Challenges

Security and resilience cannot always be addressed with a "one size fits all" approach.

Traditional security practices – such as guns, gates, and guards – while appropriate for some sectors, are not practical in others, for example:

- Where accessibility is important, such as in lodging and shopping venues.
- Where critical infrastructure is spread over large distances, such as open farmland or communications networks.

Each sector tailors its recommended security and resilience measures to its own unique environment.

Sector-Specific Solutions

In sectors where implementing protective measures provides a challenge, sector-specific training and awareness materials identify means by which security and resilience can be improved.

For example, the Commercial Facilities Sector provides access to training on surveillance detection and bomb-making awareness for employees. Materials such as these identify protective steps that owners and operators can take and are tailored specifically to a particular sector's needs.

Additional sector-specific training and awareness materials will be identified in the following lesson on information sharing.

Establishing Partnership Goals

The next step in forming partnerships is to establish specific critical infrastructure partnership goals that are not currently met under existing hazard mitigation, emergency management, or other programs.

When establishing goals, it is important to understand the value proposition resulting from partnerships.

The risk management process also may identify specific infrastructure protection needs (for example, a need for current threat/hazard information) that inform partnership goals. Risk management is covered in the following lesson.

Partnership Goals

Goals that are collaboratively derived help maintain a common vision of desired long-term security posture and resilience criteria.

Critical infrastructure goals identified during the collaborative planning process should reflect the broad security and resilience goals of the full range of partners.

Critical infrastructure partners also can draw on these goals during risk management to best determine which specific risk-reduction and protective strategies most significantly enhance preparedness in the area.

Coordinating Protective Activities

Critical infrastructure security and resilience officials within a jurisdiction are responsible for coordinating security and recovery activities among regional, local, and private sector partners.

This responsibility includes ensuring that funding priorities are identified and that resources are allocated effectively to achieve critical infrastructure security and resilience goals and build capabilities in accordance with relevant plans and strategies.

Resources

Select the links below for additional information relating to the content of this lesson.

Checklists and Information Sheets

- Critical Infrastructure Security and Resilience Activities Checklists
- Emergency Management Partnership Examples
- Information Sharing: Practices That Can Benefit Critical Infrastructure Security and Resilience
- Protected Critical Infrastructure Information (PCII) Frequently Asked Questions

Web Pages

- Critical Infrastructure Security Web site
- Critical Infrastructure Resources
- Office of Infrastructure Protection (DHS) Web site
- State, Local, Tribal, and Territorial Government Coordinating Council (SLTTGCC)

Lesson Summary

In this lesson, you learned about engaging stakeholders in partnerships to protect critical infrastructure.

In the next lesson, you will learn about the importance of and methods for sharing critical infrastructure security and resilience information with stakeholders.

Lesson 3: Sharing Information

Lesson Overview

This lesson describes the importance of and resources for sharing information with critical infrastructure partners.

Upon completing this lesson, you should be able to:

- Describe the importance of sharing information with critical infrastructure partners.
- Describe critical infrastructure security and resilience information-sharing activities.
- Identify information-sharing resources.
- Identify the importance of assessing and validating information.

Critical Infrastructure Security and Resilience

Multidirectional information sharing between government and owners and operators forms the backbone of our Nation's critical infrastructure security and resilience efforts.

The importance of providing timely and accurate alerts and warning and encouraging proactive reporting of suspicious activities is demonstrated by several attempts in the recent past to purchase chemicals or other materials that can be used to make explosives. In a few critical instances, retail personnel reported their suspicions to law enforcement and thwarted a potential attack.

The suppliers of these materials were not limited to laboratory and chemical supply companies. They also include retail outlets such as home improvement stores, beauty supply stores, drug stores, and grocery stores.

The law enforcement officers investigating these incidents have found that the targets for the explosives include critical infrastructure, such as electrical power stations, reservoirs, hydroelectric dams, nuclear power plants, and other facilities.

Because the cases have not come to trial, details cannot be provided here.

Nonetheless, they demonstrate how information sharing between government officials and owners and operators plays a crucial role in protecting our critical infrastructure.

Information sharing by government partners identifies what should be reported and to whom. As a result, there were procedures already in place to report suspicious activities.

In turn, the owners and operators in these incidents shared their information about suspicious activities with their law enforcement partners.

Without information sharing from both directions, the results could have been much different.

Sharing Information

The third critical infrastructure security and resilience activity is sharing information.

Information sharing between government and critical infrastructure owners and operators is vital to protect our critical infrastructure.

Multidirectional Communications

Critical infrastructure security and resilience are dependent on multidirectional communications between all levels of government and owners and operators.

This multidirectional exchange of information provides government and owner/operator decisionmakers with the information they need to:

- Develop and implement effective critical infrastructure security and resilience programs.
- Respond to and recover from events that threaten critical infrastructure.

Information-Sharing Roles for Government

Governments, primarily from Federal, State, and major urban levels:

- Provide information on threats and hazards to enable owners and operators to protect critical infrastructure.
- Provide information on mechanisms and procedures for reporting real-time suspicious activities and threats to the appropriate authorities.

Officials at all levels of government ensure that this information reaches critical infrastructure owners and operators.

Information-Sharing Roles for Owners and Operators

Owners and operators:

- Provide information on vulnerabilities and other information that will assist in managing risk.
- Provide information on real-time suspicious activities or other threats/hazards occurring at their locations.

Information-Sharing Activities

Recommended information-sharing activities for officials with critical infrastructure include:

- Determining information needs to maintain situational awareness and implement security and resilience programs.
- Identifying your information assets and sources (those currently available or needed).
- Establishing mechanisms for collecting and checking information.
- Making information available to share.

This checklist provides recommended critical infrastructure security and resilience information-sharing activities for State, local, tribal, and territorial (SLTT) governments.

- ☐ Determine information needs to maintain situational awareness and protect critical infrastructure. Ask:

    - ☐ What questions am I trying to answer (who, what, when, where, how)?
    - ☐ Why do I need this information?
    - ☐ What am I going to do with this information?

- ☐ Identify information assets (what you currently have or collect) and determine what you can through your own research.
- ☐ Identify other information sources to meet needs.
- ☐ Facilitate the sharing of real-time threat and incident information through partnerships and information-sharing mechanisms.
- ☐ Establish mechanisms for collecting information from critical infrastructure employees and others, identifying:

    - ☐ How to encourage participation.
    - ☐ How to capture reported information.

- ☐ How to validate reported information (see below).
- ☐ How to forward information.

☐ Check collected information for reliability and validity/accuracy.

- ☐ Assess reliability of the source by asking:
    - ☐ Does the source have a history of reliability?
    - ☐ Are there any doubts about the source's competency?
    - ☐ Are there any doubts about the trustworthiness of the source?
    - ☐ Was the source in a position to accurately observe the information?
- ☐ Double-check the facts. Assess validity/accuracy of the information by asking:
    - ☐ Can the information be confirmed by other independent sources?
    - ☐ Is the information logical?
    - ☐ Is the information consistent with other information?
    - ☐ Are there contradictions in the information that need to be addressed?

☐ Share critical infrastructure information to enable prioritized security and restoration of critical public services, facilities, utilities, and functions within the jurisdiction.

Determining Information Needs

The first step in the information-sharing process is for all critical infrastructure stakeholders to determine the information that is needed to protect critical infrastructure.

The identification of information needs:

- Supports identification of threats and hazards.
- Focuses information-collection efforts.
- Enables critical infrastructure partners to obtain a common operating picture.
- Supports decisionmakers in making informed judgments.

In order to determine information needs, you should ask:

- What questions am I trying to answer (who, what, when, where, how)?
- Why do I need this information?
- What am I going to do with this information?

When identifying the questions that need to be answered by critical infrastructure stakeholders, keep in mind:

- External (e.g., regulatory requirements) critical infrastructure security and resilience reporting requirements, and
- Grant and program application requirements.

Information-Sharing Example

The cities of Portland, Oregon, and Vancouver, Washington, asked critical infrastructure owners and operators to complete surveys identifying the potential impact from a worst-case scenario (in which everything has gone wrong).

The scenarios involved damage, impairment, and hostile takeover of a critical infrastructure asset or facility.

The information from the Portland/Vancouver surveys:

- Helped to identify specific critical infrastructure security and resilience concerns from owners and operators.
- Played an important role in designing tabletop exercises for a workshop that explored interdependencies between the sectors within the geographic area.

Identifying Information Resources

After information needs have been determined, the next step is to identify where and how you can find the information to meet those needs.

Information resources include the mechanisms and systems that you use to obtain the information you need.

Communities of Interest

Public-private partnerships, such as critical infrastructure sector communities of interest, provide several mechanisms for sharing information.

Communities of interest are partnerships organized by State organizations, Federal organizations, or mission areas such as emergency management, law enforcement, critical infrastructure, or intelligence.

Within the Homeland Security Information Network – Critical Infrastructure (HSIN-CI) Web portal, users can securely share within their communities or reach out to other communities as needed.

Accessing the Homeland Security Information Network (HSIN)

The Homeland Security Information Network (HSIN) is a national secure and trusted Web-based portal for information sharing and collaboration between Federal, State, local, tribal, territorial, private-sector, and international partners engaged in the homeland security mission.

HSIN is made up of a growing network of communities, called communities of interest (COIs). HSIN provides secure, real-time collaboration tools, including a virtual meeting space, instant messaging and document sharing. HSIN allows partners to work together instantly, regardless of their location, to communicate, collaborate, and coordinate.

For information regarding the HSIN – Critical Infrastructure (HSIN-CI) program or to gain access, please email HSIN.Outreach@hq.dhs.gov. If requesting access, please indicate which sector(s) you wish to join and include your name, official e-mail address, organization, supervisor's name, and a phone number.

Other Public-Private Information-Sharing Resources

In addition to HSIN-CI, other information-sharing resources associated with public-private partnerships include:

- InfraGard (FBI-organized public-private partnership network).
- Lessons Learned Information Sharing (LLIS).

Trade associations and critical infrastructure sectors also may offer other means of obtaining information relating to critical infrastructure security and resilience.

In addition to HSIN-CI, other information-sharing resources associated with public-private partnerships include:

- InfraGard (FBI-organized public-private partnership network).
- Lessons Learned Information Sharing (LLIS).

Trade associations and critical infrastructure sectors also may offer other means of obtaining information relating to critical infrastructure security and resilience.

Public-Private Partnership Resources

InfraGard®

InfraGard is an information-sharing and analysis effort serving the interests and combining the knowledge base of a wide range of members. At its most basic level, InfraGard is a partnership between the FBI and the private sector. InfraGard is an association of businesses, academic institutions, State and local law enforcement agencies, and other participants dedicated to sharing information and intelligence to prevent hostile acts against the United States.

InfraGard members gain access to information that enables them to protect their assets and in turn provide information to the Government that facilitates its responsibilities to prevent and address terrorism and other crimes.

For more information about InfraGard and to apply for membership, refer to the InfraGard Web site at http://www.infragard.net.

Lessons Learned Information Sharing (LLIS)

The Lessons Learned Information Sharing (LLIS) program is part of FEMA's National Preparedness Assessment Division (NPAD). NPAD's mission is to advance all hazards preparedness by assessing and communicating investments, activities, and accomplishments related to national preparedness. The LLIS program supports this mission by:

- Developing and disseminating lessons learned, innovative practices, and other related content to support continuous improvement throughout the whole community;
- Analyzing emergency management capabilities in order to identify common areas of strengths or improvements; and
- Developing policy and doctrine.

Information-Sharing and Fusion Centers

Information-sharing and fusion centers provide time-sensitive threat information for their area of responsibility. They coordinate the collection, analysis, and dissemination of law enforcement, homeland security, public safety, and terrorism information for a region or sector.

Examples include:

State and Major Urban Fusion Centers

State and major urban fusion centers (fusion centers) serve as focal points within the State and local environment for the receipt, analysis, gathering, and sharing of threat-related information between the Federal Government and State, local, tribal, and territorial (SLTT) and private-sector partners.

Located in States and major urban areas throughout the country, fusion centers are uniquely situated to empower front-line law enforcement, public safety, fire service, emergency response, public health, critical infrastructure security and resilience, and private-sector security personnel to understand local implications of national intelligence, thus enabling local officials to better protect their communities. Fusion centers provide interdisciplinary expertise and situational awareness to inform decisionmaking at all levels of government. They conduct analysis and facilitate information sharing while assisting law enforcement and homeland security partners in preventing, protecting against, and responding to crime and terrorism.

Fusion centers are owned and operated by State and local entities with support from Federal partners in the form of deployed personnel, training, technical assistance, exercise support, security clearances, connectivity to Federal systems, technology, and grant funding.

Fusion center contact information is maintained by the National Fusion Center Association at http://www.nfcausa.org.

Regional Information Sharing System (RISS)® and Automated Trusted Information Exchange (ATIX)™

RISS is a national program composed of six regional intelligence centers, operating in unique multistate geographic regions. RISS offers services to local, State, Federal, and tribal law enforcement and criminal justice agencies to enhance their ability to identify, target, and remove criminal conspiracies and activities spanning multijurisdictional, multistate and, sometimes, international boundaries.

RISS supports investigation and prosecution efforts against terrorism, drug trafficking, human trafficking, identity theft, cybercrime, organized criminal activity, criminal gangs, violent crime, and other regional priorities, while promoting officer safety. RISS provides information-sharing services, investigative analysis support, equipment sharing, investigative funds support, training, and technical assistance to law enforcement and criminal justice agencies that are members of RISS.

RISS launched the Automated Trusted Information Exchange (ATIX) to expand communication and information sharing to public safety and private-sector officials. RISS ATIX is a communications system that allows authorized users to share terrorism and homeland security information in a secure, real-time environment.

Participants are designated into specific communities based on their role regarding the prevention, response, mitigation, and recovery efforts related to disasters or other public safety or law enforcement efforts. RISS ATIX communities include executives and officials from local, county, State, and tribal governments, representatives of emergency management and law enforcement entities, and other entities involved in local and national security or disaster recovery efforts, such as nongovernmental entities, private security, and critical sector entities.

If you are an official or executive staff member from a governmental or nongovernmental entity involved with planning and implementing prevention, response, mitigation, and recovery efforts regarding disasters or other public safety and law enforcement efforts, contact your in-region RISS Center (http://www.riss.net/Centers/Centers) for additional information about how to connect to ATIX.

Information Sharing and Analysis Centers

The goal of Information Sharing and Analysis Centers (ISACs) is to provide users with accurate, actionable, and relevant information within a particular critical infrastructure sector.

Services provided by ISACs include risk mitigation, incident response, alert and information sharing. Member benefits vary across the ISACs and can include: access to a 24/7 security operations center, briefings, white papers, threat calls, webinars, and anonymous owner/operator reporting.

Critical infrastructure owners and operators, through the ISAC, can share and analyze physical and cyber infrastructure protection information within the particular sector. The ISAC's analyses are shared within the sector, with other sectors, and with government.

For more information on Information Sharing and Analysis Centers and a list of the ISACs, refer to the National Council of ISACs Web page (http://www.isaccouncil.org).

National Terrorism Advisory System (NTAS) Alerts

The National Terrorism Advisory System replaces the color-coded Homeland Security Advisory System.

NTAS alerts are issued when credible threat information is available. The alerts will provide a concise summary of the potential threat, information about actions being taken to ensure public safety, and recommended steps that individuals, communities, businesses, and governments can take to help prevent, mitigate, or respond to the threat.

For more information about receiving National Terrorism Advisory alerts, refer to the official NTAS webpage (http://www.dhs.gov/alerts).

National Weather Service Advisories and Warnings

The National Weather Service is tasked with providing weather, hydrologic, and climate forecasts and warnings for the protection of life and property.

The National Weather Service issues warnings when the following types of events are occurring, imminent, or likely:

- Extreme weather events, to include hurricanes, cyclones, tropical storms, and tornadoes.
- Potential for flooding.
- Potential for wildfires.
- High seas (coastal).

Reporting Critical Infrastructure Security and Resilience Information

The flow of information from various sources to the appropriate response and protection authorities is essential to critical infrastructure security and resilience programs.

This includes information needed for:

- Regulatory and infrastructure protection reporting (e.g., threat and hazard identification and risk assessment reporting, critical infrastructure inventories, grant program reporting, and other requirements).
- Vulnerability assessment reports.

Reporting Potential Threat Information

Information-sharing processes need to identify channels for reporting potential threats to the appropriate officials, such as through existing emergency and law enforcement reporting systems.

These reports:

- Alert officials to initiate investigations and begin response procedures as appropriate.
- Identify activities that may be part of a larger threat, such as surveillance activities across a number of sectors or in a broader geographical area.

If You See Something, Say Something™

The DHS public awareness campaign, "If You See Something, Say Something™," helps to emphasize the importance of reporting suspicious information.

Communities throughout the United States are placing posters in public transportation systems and using organizations such as neighborhood watch groups to promote the "If You See Something, Say Something™" campaign.

Critical infrastructure owners and operators are encouraged to post in prominent locations contact information, such as local police phone numbers, to report suspicious activities.

If You See Something, Say Something.

Report Suspicious Activity to Local Law Enforcement or Call 911.

In July 2010, the Department of Homeland Security (DHS), at Secretary Janet Napolitano's direction, launched a national "If You See Something, Say Something™" public awareness campaign –a simple and effective program to raise public awareness of indicators of terrorism and violent crime, and to emphasize the importance of reporting suspicious activity to the proper State and local law enforcement authorities. The campaign was originally used by New York's Metropolitan Transportation Authority (MTA), which has licensed the use of the slogan to DHS for antiterrorism and anticrime efforts.

A critical element of the DHS mission is ensuring that the civil rights and civil liberties of persons are not diminished by our security efforts, activities, and programs. Consequently, the "If You See Something, Say Something™" campaign respects civil rights and civil liberties by emphasizing behavior, rather than appearance, in identifying suspicious activity.

Factors such as race, ethnicity, national origin, or religious affiliation alone are not suspicious. For that reason, the public should report only suspicious behavior and situations (e.g., an unattended backpack in a public place or someone trying to break into a restricted area) rather than beliefs, thoughts, ideas, expressions, associations, or speech unrelated to terrorism or other criminal activity. Only reports that document **behavior reasonably indicative of criminal activity related to terrorism** will be shared with Federal partners.

The "If You See Something, Say Something™" campaign was launched in conjunction with the rollout of the Nationwide Suspicious Activity Reporting Initiative (NSI). The NSI is an administration-wide effort to develop, evaluate, and implement common processes and policies for gathering, documenting, processing, analyzing, and sharing information about terrorism-related suspicious activities. Led by the Department of Justice, the NSI is implemented in partnership with State and local officials across the Nation.

Both the "If You See Something, Say Something™" campaign and the NSI underscore the concept that homeland security begins with hometown security, where an alert public plays a critical role in keeping our Nation safe.

To date, DHS has launched "If You See Something, Say Something™" with: Amtrak; the general aviation community; the Washington, DC Metropolitan Police Department; the Colorado Rockies, the Indianapolis 500, the Washington Metropolitan Area Transit Authority; the Pentagon Force Protection Agency; the U.S. Tennis Association; a variety of States including six States participating in the Southern Shield that joined the NSI – Tennessee, Virginia, Alabama, Georgia, South Carolina, and Florida; the New York Mets; Meadowlands Stadium; the American Hotel and Lodging Association; New Jersey Transit; the Mall of America; Wal-Mart; the National Football League; the National Basketball Association; AEG Facilities; the National Collegiate Athletic Association; and all Federal buildings across the country protected by the Federal Protective Service.

DHS will continue to roll out the campaign to numerous additional States and partners in the private sector.

"If You See Something, Say Something™" is used with permission of the NY Metropolitan Transportation Authority.

Nationwide Suspicious Activity Reporting Initiative

The Nationwide Suspicious Activity Reporting Initiative (NSI) is a Federal administration-wide effort to develop and implement common processes and policies for gathering, documenting, processing, analyzing, and sharing information about terrorism-related suspicious activities. It was launched in conjunction with the "If You See Something, Say Something™" campaign.

Select this link for additional information about the NSI.

Collecting and Verifying Information

With any system of information, the details that are reported need to be assessed and validated. This is the next step of information sharing.

There are two ways in which reported information should be evaluated:

- By the reliability of the source.
- By the validity of the information.

Evaluating the Reliability of the Source

When evaluating the reliability of the source, ask questions such as:

- Does the source have a history of reliability?
- Are there any doubts about the competency or trustworthiness of the source?
- Was the source in a position to accurately observe the information?

Evaluating the Validity of the Information

When evaluating the validity of the information, ask questions such as:

- Can the information be confirmed by other independent sources?
- Is the information logical?
- Is the information consistent with other information?
- Are there contradictions in the information that need to be addressed?

Making Information Available

The last step in the information-sharing process is making information available to other critical infrastructure partners.

This includes:

- Information about current and threats and hazards.
- Information that will assist in identifying critical infrastructure vulnerabilities.

Resources

Select the links below for additional information relating to the content of this lesson.

Information Sheets

- Critical Infrastructure Security and Resilience Activities Checklists
- "If You See Something, Say Something™" Campaign
- Information-Sharing Resources
- Nationwide Suspicious Activity Reporting Initiative (NSI)

Web Pages

- Critical Infrastructure Security Web site
- Critical Infrastructure Training
- Critical Infrastructure Resources
- Fusion Center Contact Information
- Homeland Security Information Network (HSIN) Communities of Interest
- "If You See Something, Say Something™" Campaign
- InfraGard
- Lessons Learned Information Sharing
- Multi-State Information Sharing & Analysis Center (MS-ISAC)
- National Council of Information Sharing and Analysis Centers (ISACs) Web Site
- Nationwide Suspicious Activity Reporting (SAR) Initiative
- Office of Infrastructure Protection (DHS) Web Site
- Regional Information Sharing System/Anti-Terrorism Information Exchange

Lesson Summary

In this lesson, you learned about the information-sharing process, reviewed key information resources for critical infrastructure security and resilience, and learned the importance of verifying information.

In the next lesson, you will learn about managing risk.

Lesson 4: Managing Risk

Lesson Overview

This lesson presents an overview of processes and resources for managing risk to critical infrastructure.

Upon completing this lesson, you should be able to:

- Describe the importance of using a risk-informed approach as the foundation of our critical infrastructure security and resilience efforts.
- Describe the basic steps of a risk management strategy.
- Identify resources that can be used to determine critical infrastructure risk management strategies.

A Risk-Informed Approach to Critical Infrastructure Security and Resilience

Brandon Wales is Director of the Homeland Infrastructure Threat and Risk Analysis Center. Recently he was asked why we use a risk-informed approach to critical infrastructure security and resilience. Mr. Wales responded as follows:

We work in a field that has a lot of uncertainty. We don't know where the next terrorist attack will happen, if any. We don't know where the next natural hazard will hit the country.

And given that uncertainty, we need some way to help us identify where we should be putting our energy, our resources, our national attention, our national focus, the attention of our State and local partners, and the attention of our interagency partners.

The way we do that is through a risk assessment process. Risk assessments help us to use whatever information we do have and craft the best possible answer to the question, "How do we use limited resources to better protect our country and to help it respond to incidents?"

Mr. Wales concluded by saying that, in many cases, risk assessment provides the **only** answers to the question, "How do I spend my limited resources when we don't have a lot of information on the next possible target or disaster?"

What Is Risk?

Risk is the potential for an unwanted outcome resulting from an incident, event, or occurrence as determined by its likelihood and the associated consequences. It is a function of threat/hazard, vulnerability, and consequences.

Risk is influenced by:

- The nature and magnitude of the **threat/hazard** (the greater the threat/hazard, the greater the risk).
- The **vulnerabilities** to that threat/hazard (the more vulnerable you are, the greater the risk).
- The **consequences** that could result if the threat/hazard is realized (the higher the consequences, the greater the risk).

Managing Risk

The fourth critical infrastructure security and resilience activity is managing risk.

Risk management identifies how:

- **Threats and hazards** will be deterred.
- **Vulnerabilities** will be mitigated.
- **Consequences** will be minimized.

As indicated by Mr. Wales in the video, your risk assessment identifies where best to put sometimes limited resources to better protect our critical infrastructure.

Risk management measures also may include the means for improving resilience and enabling timely, efficient response and restoration in a post-event situation.

Presidential Policy Directive/PPD-8: National Preparedness

PPD-8 establishes a vision for the whole community—including individuals, businesses, community- and faith-based organizations, schools, tribes and all levels of government—to work together to:

- Understand risks they face.
- Build and sustain the capabilities needed to be secure and resilient.

PPD-8 Implementation priorities include:

- National Preparedness Goal
- National Preparedness System
- Campaign to Build and Sustain Preparedness
- National Preparedness Report

Select this link to access Presidential Policy Directive/PPD-8.

National Preparedness System

The National Preparedness System, a component of PPD-8, is an integrated set of guidance, programs, and processes that comprise the following six major components:

Identifying and Assessing Risk

Developing and maintaining an understanding of the variety of risks faced by communities and the Nation, and how this information can be used to build and sustain preparedness, are essential components of the National Preparedness System. A risk assessment collects information regarding the threats and hazards, including the projected consequences or impacts.

Estimating Capability Requirements

To fully understand capability requirements, each community, organization, and level of government must consider single threats or hazards as well as the full range of risks they may face. Using the results from a risk assessment in the context of the desired outcome(s) for each mission area, the required types and levels of capability can be estimated.

Building and Sustaining Capabilities

After completing the estimation process, existing and needed capabilities can be analyzed and gaps identified. These gaps can be prioritized based on a combination of the desired outcomes, risk assessments, and the effects of not addressing the gaps.

Working together, planners, government officials, and elected leaders can develop strategies to allocate resources effectively, as well as leverage available assistance to reduce risk. These strategies consider how to both sustain current levels of capability and address gaps in order to achieve the National Preparedness Goal.

Planning to Deliver Capabilities

The whole community contributes to reducing the Nation's risks. Planning for low-probability, high-consequence risks—such as a terrorist attack with nuclear or biological weapons or a catastrophic earthquake affecting multiple jurisdictions—will be a complex undertaking and involve many partners. Federal efforts, therefore, must complement planning at other levels of government, which is often focused on more likely risks. These shared planning efforts form a National Planning System by which the whole community can think through crises, determine capability requirements, and address the collective risk identified during the risk assessment process.

Validating Capabilities

Measuring progress toward achieving the National Preparedness Goal will provide the means to decide how and where to allocate scarce resources and prioritize preparedness. This validation process can be done through exercises, remedial action management programs, and assessments.

Reviewing and Updating

The Nation's security and resilience will be strengthened as it employs the components of the National Preparedness System. Changes in a community's exposure and sensitivity can and do occur, however, whether from evolving threats and hazards, aging infrastructure, shifts in population, or changes in the natural environment. On a recurring basis, capabilities, resources, and plans should be reviewed to determine if they remain relevant or need to be updated.

Risk Management Framework

The model used for managing risk to critical infrastructure appears below. Jurisdictions along with owners and operators use this system to manage risks to critical infrastructure assets, systems, and networks.

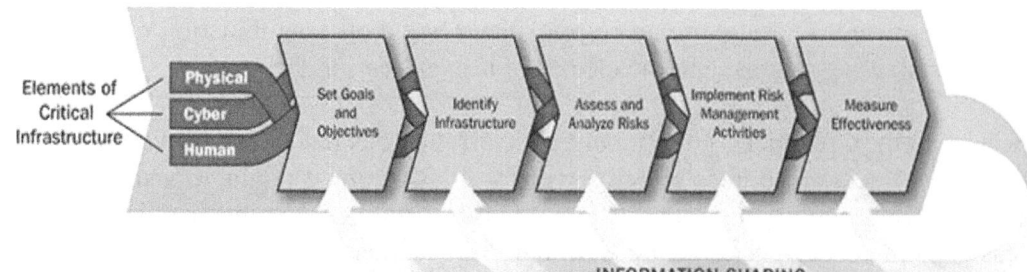

The cornerstone of the NIPP is its risk management framework that establishes the processes for combining consequence, vulnerability, and threat/hazard information to produce a comprehensive, systematic, and rational assessment of national or sector risk. The risk management framework is structured to promote continuous improvement to enhance critical infrastructure security and resilience by focusing activities on efforts to:

- **Set Goals and Objectives:** Define specific outcomes, conditions, end points, or performance targets that collectively constitute an effective protective posture.
- **Identify Infrastructure:** Develop an inventory of the critical infrastructure assets, systems, and networks.
- **Assess and Analyze Risks:** Determine risk by combining direct and indirect consequences of a terrorist attack or other hazards, known vulnerabilities to various attack vectors, and general or specific threat/hazard information.
- **Implement Risk Management Activities:** Select sector-appropriate protective actions or programs to reduce or manage the risk identified and secure the resources needed to address priorities.
- **Measure Effectiveness:** Use metrics and other evaluation procedures at the national and sector levels to measure progress and assess the effectiveness of the critical infrastructure security and resilience program in improving protection, managing risk, and increasing resilience.

NIPP 2013 Supplement: Executing a Critical Infrastructure Risk Management Approach

Risk is defined as the potential for an unwanted outcome resulting from an incident, event, or occurrence, as determined by its likelihood and the associated consequences1. It is influenced by the nature and magnitude of a threat or hazard, the vulnerabilities from that threat or hazard, and the consequences that could result. Risk information allows partners, from facility owners and operators to Federal agencies, to prioritize risk management efforts.

This supplement describes a useful critical infrastructure risk management approach, which supports the risk management framework depicted in Figure 1. The framework enables the integration of strategies, capabilities, and governance structures to enable risk-informed decision making related to the Nation's critical infrastructure. The critical infrastructure risk management approach described in this supplement can be applied to all threats and hazards, including cyber incidents, natural disasters, man-made safety hazards, and acts of terrorism, although different information and methodologies may be used to understand each.

Select this link to access a copy of NIPP 2013 Supplement: Executing a Critical Infrastructure Risk Management Approach

Risk in the Context of National Preparedness

PPD-8 creates the National Preparedness Goal and System which describe five mission areas that provide a useful framework for considering risk management investments. The graphic titled "Critical Infrastructure Risk in the Context of National Preparedness" illustrates the relationship of the national preparedness mission areas to the elements of risk.

- Prevention activities are most closely associated with efforts to address threats;
- Protection efforts generally address vulnerabilities; and
- Response and Recovery efforts help minimize consequences.
- Mitigation efforts transcend the entire threat, vulnerability, and consequence spectrum.

The National Preparedness Goal also establishes 31 core capabilities that support the five national preparedness mission areas. The NIPP is aligned with PPD-8, and the PPD-8 mission areas are central to a comprehensive approach for enhancing national preparedness and critical infrastructure risk management activities. The development of these capabilities contributes to achieving secure and resilient critical infrastructure; additionally, the capabilities can be applied to identify risk management activities.

Such efforts are enhanced when critical infrastructure risks are considered as part of setting capability targets.

Select this link to enlarge "Critical Infrastructure Risk in the Context of National Preparedness"

Threat and Hazard Identification and Risk Assessment

Threat and Hazard Identification and Risk Assessment, or "THIRA," provides a comprehensive approach for identifying and assessing risks and associated impacts. It is important to:

- Determine if your jurisdiction has completed the THIRA process. If so, consider the results when assessing risks to critical infrastructure.
- Consult the THIRA Guide for guidance that is applicable to analyzing critical infrastructure.

Select this link to access Comprehensive Preparedness Guide (CPG 201: Threat and Hazard Identification and Risk Assessment Guide).

Identifying Threats and Hazards

The first step in managing the risk to critical infrastructure is to identify the threats and hazards.

Identifying threats and hazards is:

- Based on past experience, forecasting, expert judgment, and available resources.
- Necessary in order determine vulnerabilities and assess consequences.

Information Sharing

The previous lesson makes the point that critical infrastructure security and resilience are dependent on multidirectional communication between owners and operators and government regarding:

- Information about threats and hazards affecting critical infrastructure.
- Information about critical infrastructure vulnerabilities.

NIPP 2013 Supplement: Connecting to the NICC and the NCCIC

This supplement describes how partners throughout the critical infrastructure community-owners and operators; Federal partners; regional consortia; and State, local, tribal, and territorial governments-can connect to the National Infrastructure Coordinating Center (NICC) and National Cybersecurity and Communications Integration Center (NCCIC). It describes the information desired by the centers and their partners, as well as how the centers protect and analyze data to inform prevention, protection, mitigation, response, and recovery activities.

Select this link to access a copy of NIPP 2013 Supplement: Connecting to the NICC and the NCCIC

Types of Threats and Hazards

Communities face a variety of threats and hazards that can be the result of natural, technological, or human-caused incidents.

- **Natural threats and hazards** are those resulting from acts of nature, such as hurricanes, earthquakes, or tornadoes and disease outbreaks or epidemics.
- **Technological threats and hazards** are those resulting from accidents or the failures of systems and structures, such as hazardous materials spills or dam failures.
- **Human-caused threats and hazards** are those resulting from the intentional actions of an adversary, such as a threatened or actual chemical or biological attack or cyber event

Types of Threats and Hazards: Examples

Natural	Technological	Human-Caused
Results from acts of nature - Avalanche - Disease outbreak - Drought - Earthquake - Epidemic - Flood - Hurricane - Landslide - Tornado - Tsunami - Volcanic eruption - Wildfire - Winter storm	**Involves accidents or the failures of systems and structures** - Airplane crash - Dam/levee failure - Hazardous materials release - Power failure - Radiological release - Train derailment - Urban conflagration	**Caused by the intentional actions of an adversary** - Civil disturbance - Cyber incidents - Sabotage - School violence - Terrorist acts

Threats From Terrorism

DHS provides its partners with Federal Government-coordinated unclassified assessments of potential terrorist threats using the information-sharing mechanisms described in the previous lesson, such as the National Terrorism Advisory System (NTAS) or the Homeland Security Information Network (HSIN).

The threat assessments are derived from analyses of adversary intent and capability and include:

- A broad view of the potential threat and postulated terrorist attack methods.

- Information about terrorist interest in particular infrastructure sectors, as well as specific attack methods.

Sources of Threat and Hazard Information

In addition to government terrorism assessments, the following sources will identify threats and hazards:

- Existing risk assessments, such as Threat and Hazard Identification and Risk Assessments (THIRAs) or Hazard Identification and Risk Assessments prepared by the States, major urban areas, and other government entities.
- Online data resources, such as U.S. Geological Survey and National Oceanic and Atmospheric Administration resources.
- Other sources, such as local fire, police, and health departments and infrastructure owners and operators.

Threat and Hazard Information Resources

Online Data Resources include:

- U.S. Geological Survey (USGS)
- National Oceanic and Atmospheric Administration (NOAA)
- Census Bureau
- FEMA Disasters and Maps
- Full-Spectrum Risk Knowledgebase
- Lessons Learned Information System (LLIS)
- Nuclear Regulatory Commission (NRC)
- National Counterterrorism Center (NCTC)
- National Institutes of Standards and Technology (NIST)
- Environmental Protection Agency (EPA)

Other sources of data and information include:

- Other existing risk assessments
- Urban Areas Security Initiative (UASI) programs
- Emergency management/homeland security agencies
- Local and State Hazard Mitigation offices
- Local National Weather Services
- FEMA regional offices
- Local fire, police, and health departments
- State and Major Urban Area Fusion Centers
- Infrastructure owners and operators

- DHS Protective Security Advisors
- Colleges and universities

Assessing Vulnerabilities and Consequences

The next step of the risk management process is to assess vulnerabilities and potential consequences to critical infrastructure in the context of human-caused threats and other hazards.

Managing risk means that we prioritize:

- The threats and hazards with the greatest impact on a jurisdiction's or organization's core capabilities.
- The threats and hazards with the greatest consequences should they occur.

Vulnerability Assessment Methodologies

A wide variety of methods can be used to assess vulnerabilities, several of which are described in this module.

Whatever method is used, it is important to assess all potential vulnerabilities within a critical infrastructure asset, system, or network and to map dependencies and interdependencies, for example:

- The impact of a lack of fuel for a critical component within a system.
- The point at which an event affects the ability of critical personnel to report to work.

Cross-Sector Interdependencies and Risk Management

Cross-sector interdependencies should be considered when conducting risk management activities and developing critical infrastructure security and resilience programs. Security and resilience measures should include backup systems, such as alternate power sources.

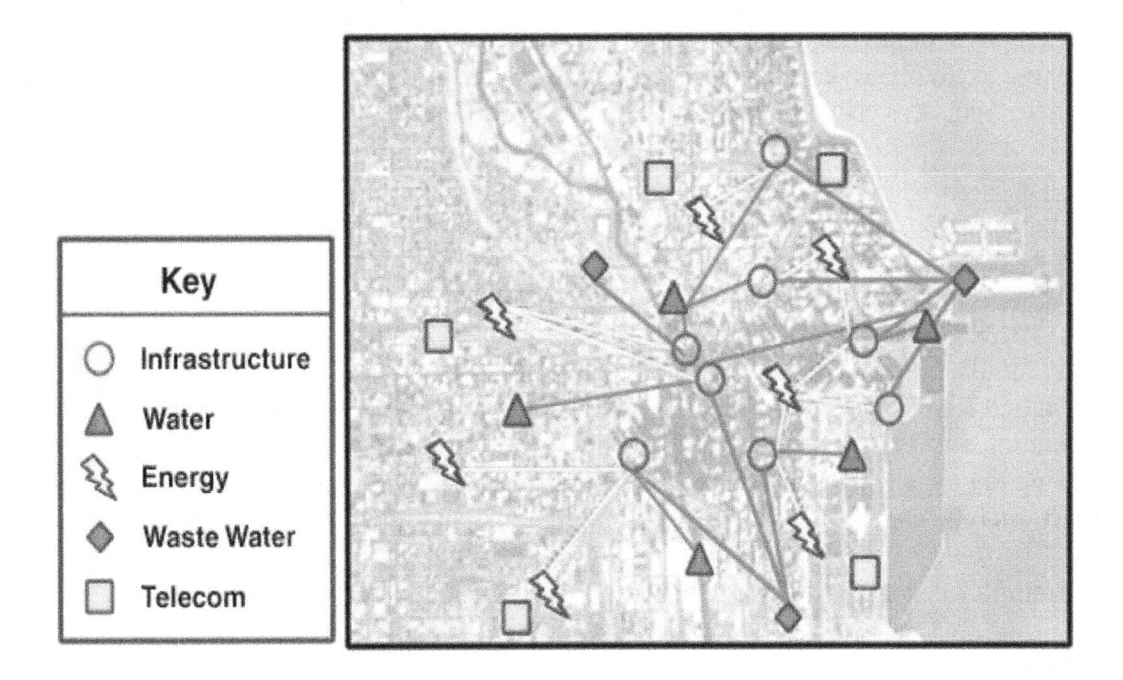

Risk and Vulnerability Assessment Resources

There are a wide variety of resources to support risk assessments, such as:

- NIPP 2013 Supplement: National Protection and Programs Directorate Resources to Support Vulnerability Assessments
- Office of Cyber & Infrastructure Analysis (OCIA)
- Critical infrastructure vulnerability assessments.
- Critical infrastructure vulnerability and protective measures reports.

Some of the resources also help owners and operators to identify protective measures.

NIPP 2013 Supplement: National Protection and Programs Directorate Resources to Support Vulnerability Assessments

Assessing vulnerabilities of critical infrastructure is an important step in developing security solutions and managing critical infrastructure risk. The Department of Homeland Security's (DHS) National Protection and Programs Directorate (NPPD) works with owners and operators to conduct vulnerability assessments of select critical infrastructure to inform its internal risk management processes and provide technical assistance to its State, local, tribal, and and territorial (SLTT) and private sector partners to enable their own risk assessments and security plans. NPPD provides additional resources, typically in the form of informational material on known vulnerabilities, to help owners and operators understand vulnerabilities at a more general level.

This supplement provides information on Federal resources that are used by DHS and available to SLTT governments and critical infrastructure owners and operators to identify and assess critical infrastructure vulnerabilities.

Select this link to access a copy of NIPP 2013 Supplement: National Protection and Programs Directorate Resources to Support Vulnerability Assessments

Office of Cyber & Infrastructure Analysis (OCIA)

OCIA builds on the recent accomplishments of the Department's Homeland Infrastructure Threat and Risk Analysis Center (HITRAC) and manages the National Infrastructure Simulation and Analysis Center (NISAC) to advance understanding of emerging risks crossing the cyber-physical domain. OCIA represents an integration and enhancement of DHS's analytic capabilities, supporting stakeholders and interagency partners.

Informing Decisions through Integrated Analysis

OCIA uses all-hazards information from an array of partners to conduct consequence modeling, simulation, and analysis. OCIA's core functions include:

- Providing analytic support to DHS leadership, operational components, and field personnel during steady-state and crises on emerging threats and incidents impacting the Nation's critical infrastructure;
- Assessing and informing national infrastructure risk management strategies on the likelihood and consequence of emerging and future risks; and
- Developing and enhancing capabilities to support crisis action by identifying and prioritizing infrastructure through the use of analytic tools and modeling capabilities.

To learn more about how OCIA can add value to the support and services provided to our partners in the private sector and across all levels of government, please contact OCIA@hq.dhs.gov.

Critical Infrastructure Vulnerability Assessments

Protective Security Advisors (PSAs) work with local officials and owners and operators at the regional and local levels to conduct specialized field assessments to identify vulnerabilities, interdependencies, and cascading effects of nationally significant critical infrastructure.

PSAs are trained critical infrastructure security and resilience and vulnerability mitigation subject-matter experts. They reside in the communities in which they work.

A site is selected for a vulnerability assessment if it meets any of the following criteria:

- Considered nationally significant critical infrastructure, with potential significant national or regional economic or public health effects
- Of such complexity or unique design that a site assistance visit would be beneficial
- Supports or is in close proximity to a designated National Special Security Event

A National Special Security Event is an event deemed by DHS to be an attractive target for terrorism due to visibility or political connection, such as the Super Bowl or a national political party convention.

You can request to be contacted by your local PSA by sending an email to the PSA Field Operations Branch at FOBanalyst@hq.dhs.gov.

Critical Infrastructure Vulnerability and Protective Measures Reports

For DHS Federal, State, local, tribal, territorial, and regional partners, special reports also are available on the following topics: Characteristics and Common Vulnerabilities, Potential Indicators of Terrorist Activity, and Protective Measures.

These reports identify common critical infrastructure vulnerabilities, sector-specific background information, and the types of terrorist activities that might be successful in exploiting these vulnerabilities. The reports cover all 16 critical infrastructure sectors.

To obtain copies of the special reports, send an email to: ipassessments@dhs.gov.

Implementing Protective Programs and Measures

The final step in managing risk is to implement protective actions or programs to address risks.

The prioritization process completed during planning, combined with threat/hazard assessments and assessment of vulnerabilities and consequences, helps to identify requirements for protective programs and measures as well as resilience strategies.

Some of the identified shortfalls or opportunities for improvement will be filled by owners and operators. Other shortfalls will be addressed through programs developed by each sector; in State, local, territorial, or tribal security and resilience plans; or through cross-sector or national initiatives undertaken by DHS.

Effective Protective Programs, Measures, and Strategies

Characteristics of effective protective programs, measures, and strategies include but are not limited to the following:

Comprehensive
Effective security and resilience must address the physical, cyber, and human elements of critical infrastructure as appropriate, and consider long-term, short-term, and sustainable activities. Resilience and backup processes are key components of comprehensive programs, measures, and strategies.

Coordinated
The responsibility for protecting critical infrastructure must be coordinated among:

- Owners and operators.
- State, local, tribal, territorial, and regional authorities as appropriate.
- Federal agencies, including Sector-Specific Agencies.

Cost-Effective
Effective critical infrastructure security and resilience seeks to use resources effectively by focusing on actions that offer the greatest mitigation of risk for any given expenditure.

Risk-Informed
Protective programs, measures, and strategies focus on mitigating risk. Effective security and resilience reduces the threat or hazard indirectly by making critical infrastructure less attractive targets, by lessening vulnerability, and by lowering potential consequences.

Wide Range of Programs, Measures, and Strategies

Risk management can include a wide range of programs, measures, and strategies:

- Prevention (e.g., installing screening, search, and detection systems).
- Mitigation (e.g., retrofitting structures to make them floodproof).
- Protection (e.g., hardening facilities).
- Response (e.g., developing emergency operations plans).
- Recovery/resilience (e.g., building redundancy).

Current or pending protective actions and programs may adequately address risk. If that is the case, document the fact and continue with any pending implementation plans.

Incorporating Resilience into Critical Infrastructure Projects

Resilience is "the ability to prepare for and adapt to changing conditions and withstand and recover rapidly from disruptions. Resilience includes the ability to withstand and recover from deliberate attacks, accidents, or naturally occurring threats or incidents." Resilient infrastructure systems are flexible and agile and should be able to bounce back after disruptions.

The NIPP 2013 Supplement: *Incorporating Resilience into Critical Infrastructure Projects* provides the critical infrastructure community with steps that support development decisions and investments in infrastructure that will enhance the resilience of critical infrastructure systems.

Select this link to access a copy of NIPP 2013 Supplement: Incorporating Resilience into Critical Infrastructure Projects

Resources for Identifying Infrastructure Security and Resilience Information and Practices

The resources identified below represent a sampling of those available for identifying critical infrastructure security and resilience information and practices.

Lessons Learned Information Sharing (LLIS)

The DHS/FEMA Lessons Learned Information Sharing Web site once served as a national online network of lessons learned, effective practices, and innovative ideas for the emergency management and homeland security communities. In the spring of 2015, the LLIS.gov website consolidated its content with FEMA.gov and the Homeland Security Digital Library (HSDL.org). One of the advantages of the reorganization of content is that homeland security and the emergency management communities may now find relevant information in one place.

Sponsored by FEMA and the Naval Postgraduate School's Center for Homeland Defense and Security, HSDL's public collection includes over 137,000 carefully-selected documents related to homeland security policy, strategy, and organizational management. Lessons Learned content submitted by state and local responders, including innovative practice documents, after-action reports, plans, templates, guides, and other materials, is now consolidated with this already substantial database. Trend analyses, case studies on the use of FEMA preparedness grants, and links to Webinar Wednesdays were transferred to a new Lessons Learned Information Sharing page on FEMA.gov.

The new LLIS page on FEMA.gov does not require a username and password, while documents that required a username and password to view on LLIS.gov still require a username and password to view on HSDL.org. More information on creating a HSDL account is available on the HSDL.org login page.

DHS Daily Open Source Infrastructure Report

Prepared each business day, the DHS Daily Open Source Infrastructure Report is a summary of open-source published information concerning significant critical infrastructure issues. Each daily report is divided by the critical infrastructure sectors and key assets defined in the National Infrastructure Protection Plan.

Homeland Security Information Network - Critical Infrastructure (HSIN-CI)

The Homeland Security Information Network (HSIN) is the trusted network for homeland security mission operations to share Sensitive But Unclassified (SBU) information. The Critical Infrastructure community on HSIN (HSIN-CI) is the primary system through which private sector owners and operators, DHS, and other federal, state, and local government agencies collaborate to protect the nation's critical infrastructure.

Within HSIN-CI, critical infrastructure community subscribers find security and resilience information and practice resources such as:

- Office of Cyber and Infrastructure Analysis (OCIA) products including multi-year modeling, simulation, and analysis products involving dependency and interdependency analysis required by strategic planners and policy analysts. The deliberate planned studies inform OCIA's ability to understand the potential consequences of hazards. These studies, which are scoped in advance and based on available data, define requirements for the development of modeling and analysis tools that estimate impacts on infrastructure, population, and economic activity. At the same time, OCIA responds to fast moving events with crisis action analysis of natural disasters, cyber events, intentional and unintentional human-caused disasters, and outbreaks of disease.
- Cyber Security and Communications Industry Engagement and Resilience (IER) program cyber-related critical infrastructure security and resilience partnerships products including national risk assessments, risk management, information sharing, protective programs, research and development requirements identification, incentives, and critical infrastructure sectors metrics.
- TRIPwire Community Gateway (TWCG) designed specifically for the Nation's critical infrastructure owners, operators, and private security personnel. TWCG provides expert threat analyses, reports, and relevant planning documents to help key private sector partners anticipate, identify, and prevent IED incidents.

Developing Implementation Plans

During the implementation process, critical infrastructure stakeholders develop prioritized implementation plans and incorporate implementation into existing plans as needed.

Implementation plans should include assigned tasks with deadlines and a means of charting progress in reaching milestones.

Stakeholders will implement the needed protective actions and programs according to the plan or will adjust the plan as needed.

Risk Management Activities: Summary

Knowledge of these risks allows jurisdictions and critical infrastructure owners and operators to make informed decisions about how to manage risk and develop needed capabilities.

In this lesson, the following risk management activities were presented:

- Identifying threats and hazards.
- Assessing vulnerabilities and consequences.
- Implementing protective programs and measures.

Risk Management Activities

This checklist provides recommended critical infrastructure security and resilience risk management activities for State, local, tribal, and territorial (SLTT) governments.

☐ Identify threats and hazards that could affect critical infrastructure.

- ☐ Obtain threat and hazard assessment information concerning terrorism through Federal and other appropriate channels.
- ☐ For natural disasters and accidental hazards, use best-available analytic tools and historical data to estimate the likelihood of these events.

☐ Assess vulnerabilities and consequences.

- ☐ Assess critical infrastructure vulnerabilities to identified threats and hazards.

- o ☐ Leverage existing vulnerability assessment programs and tools.
- o ☐ Incorporate completed vulnerability assessment data.
- ☐ Assess potential consequences to critical infrastructure based on identified threats/hazards and vulnerabilities.
- ☐ Incorporate dependency, interdependency, and other analyses, as needed.

☐ Implement protective programs and measures.

- ☐ Identify effective practices based on recognized industry best practices and standards.
- ☐ Leverage existing Federal and other programs. Coordinate with State, regional, and territorial representatives concerning Federal assistance and initiatives. For example:
  - o ☐ Act as a conduit for requests for Federal assistance when the threat/hazard or current situation exceeds the capabilities of the jurisdiction and the private entities resident within it.
  - o ☐ Provide information to owners and operators, as part of the grants process and/or homeland security strategy updates, regarding State priorities, requirements, and critical infrastructure funding needs.
- ☐ Identify and communicate to DHS requirements from owners and operators for research and development related to critical infrastructure.
- ☐ Develop a prioritized implementation plan.
  - o ☐ Describe assigned tasks with deadlines.
  - o ☐ Provide a means to chart progress in reaching milestones.
  - o ☐ Incorporate implementation into existing plans as needed.
- ☐ Implement programs and measures.
  - o ☐ Establish continuity plans and programs that facilitate the performance of critical functions during an emergency or until normal operations can be resumed.
  - o ☐ Provide response and protective measures, as appropriate, where there are gaps and where local entities lack the resources needed to address those gaps.

Resources

Select the links below for additional information relating to the content of this lesson.

Information Sheets

- Lessons Learned Information Sharing (LLIS)
- Risk and Vulnerability Assessment Resources

Publications

- Comprehensive Preparedness Guide (CPG) 201: Threat and Hazard Identification and Risk Assessment
- National Preparedness Goal
- National Preparedness System
- Presidential Policy Directive 8

Lesson Summary

In this lesson, you learned about the importance of using a risk-informed approach as the foundation of our critical infrastructure security and resilience efforts.

In the next lesson, you will learn how critical infrastructure security and resilience plans, policies, and procedures are developed, validated, and refined through collaborative processes for planning, testing, and exercising.

Lesson 5: Ensuring Continuous Improvement

Lesson Overview

This lesson presents an overview of how critical infrastructure security and resilience plans and measures are validated and refined through training, testing, and exercising.

Upon completing this lesson, you should be able to:

- Describe the importance of and methods for training, testing, and exercising of protective plans, policies, and procedures.
- Identify potential critical infrastructure security and resilience training resources.
- Identify resources available to develop exercises.
- Explain the importance of adding or updating critical infrastructure plans based on lessons learned from testing and exercising.

Critical Infrastructure Security and Resilience: Closing the Gaps

A critical aspect of risk management is to prepare personnel through training, testing, and improving protective measures. For example, power restoration is critical for continued operations of financial institutions, hospitals, and operations or intelligence centers. Food retailers also need immediate power restoration to freezers and coolers or risk business losses.

Following a vulnerability assessment, one community pre-positioned backup generators that operate using diesel fuel. However, fuel could not be stockpiled at the generator locations because of the risks involved.

During an exercise of the emergency plan, the community discovered that even if fuel delivery trucks could arrive at the fuel depot, the fuel pumps to fill the trucks would not operate without electrical power. The dependency of the pumps on power was not identified during the planning process, but rather during the exercise.

The solution was to acquire small electrical generators to operate the pumps using the diesel fuel on hand. As a result, a power loss will not impact diesel fuel delivery to facilities using emergency generators.

Exercising and testing of the plan helped to identify this gap in protection and resolve it. Training, exercising, and testing protective measures are the keys to prevention and recovery.

Ensuring Continuous Improvement

The final critical infrastructure security and resilience activity to be discussed in this course is ensuring continuous improvement.

This step involves a continuous cycle of training, exercising, evaluating, and improving.

The activities associated with ensuring continuous improvement serve either to validate or to identify gaps in existing plans, programs, policies, and practices.

These gaps may require training or other corrective actions that include adding or updating plans that relate to critical infrastructure security and resilience.

Continuous Improvement Activities

Activities to ensure continuous improvement include the following steps:

- Conducting training of critical infrastructure security and resilience plans, policies, and procedures.
- Conducting tests and exercises of plans, policies, and procedures.
- Documenting lessons learned from tests and exercises.
- Taking corrective actions, which may include additional or enhanced training.
- Adding or updating critical infrastructure plans.

This checklist provides recommended critical infrastructure security and resilience continuous improvement activities for State, local, tribal, and territorial (SLTT) governments.

☐ Participate in education and training offered by government and sector partners as appropriate.

- ☐ Arrange for training to be conducted in your jurisdiction as possible.
- ☐ Encourage all stakeholders to participate in training sessions.

- ☐ Participate in industry-related and professional or trade association training as needed.

    - ☐ Arrange for training to be conducted in your jurisdiction as possible.
    - ☐ Encourage all stakeholders to participate in training sessions.

- ☐ Test and practice protective measures with all stakeholders.

    - ☐ Conduct red-team testing.
    - ☐ Practice procedures.

- ☐ Participate in exercises of critical infrastructure security and resilience programs and plans.

    - ☐ Develop and conduct exercises.
    - ☐ Include critical infrastructure security and resilience in existing exercises.
    - ☐ Participate in State and regional exercises.

- ☐ Document lessons learned from predisaster mitigation efforts and testing, exercises, and actual incidents and apply that learning, where applicable, to the critical infrastructure context.
- ☐ Develop an implementation plan and take corrective actions.

    - ☐ Identify additional training needs.
    - ☐ Identify other needed actions.
    - ☐ Coordinate with other government and private-sector partners as needed to implement corrective actions.

- ☐ Add or update implementation and other plans as necessary.

    - ☐ Critical infrastructure security and resilience plans.
    - ☐ Hazard mitigation plans (also called hazard plans or mitigation plans).
    - ☐ Emergency operations or response plans.
    - ☐ Continuity of operations plans.

Conducting Training

The first step in the process is to conduct training. Training enhances preparedness by providing the following:

- A means of ensuring that government and private-sector partners and employees are:
    - Knowledgeable about threats and hazards.
    - Better prepared to protect against and respond to them.
- A mechanism to implement corrective actions identified in lessons learned reporting from testing and exercising.

Training Prepares Infrastructure Security and Resilience Partners

Training allows critical infrastructure security and resilience partners to:

- Learn about potential threats.
- Learn roles and responsibilities.
- Apply policies, plans, and procedures in a safe environment.
- Practice using systems and equipment.

Training Options

There are several options for conducting training.

Training Type	Appropriate for Providing:
Classroom training	<ul><li>A knowledge base of new or revised processes and/or procedures.</li><li>The skills needed to perform tasks using computers or other equipment.</li></ul>
Independent study	<ul><li>Knowledge acquisition at a pace that is comfortable for the learner.</li><li>An opportunity to learn and apply knowledge and skills (e.g., through a tutorial) in a self-paced environment.</li></ul>

On-the-job training	• An opportunity to learn and perform tasks in a real-life environment with the supervision of an expert performer.
Briefings	• New information, usually at a high level, to all persons who have a need to know or use the information. Briefings are often provided to large groups and include a question-and-answer session.
Seminars	• Opportunities for small numbers of job performers to discuss specific topics, usually with the advice of an expert performer. Seminars usually involve new policies, procedures, or solutions to problems being presented to the group.
Workshops	• Opportunities for small numbers of job performers to discuss issues and apply knowledge and skills to solving problems or producing a product. Workshops are generally highly structured and their outputs are usually specified in advance (e.g., a list of assumptions that will be used to develop an infrastructure protection plan).
Job aids	• Quick references that are intended to be used on the job. Common job aids include checklists, worksheets, standard operating procedures, and reference guides.

Education and Training Resources

The DHS Office of Infrastructure Protection and the Critical Infrastructure Sectors, through FEMA's Emergency Management Institute (EMI) Independent Study program and National Training and Education Division (NTED), offer training programs and resources to provide the knowledge and skills needed to identify and implement critical infrastructure security and resilience activities.

There may be additional outreach and training programs offered by other levels of government that are available in your jurisdiction.

- Select this link to access the FEMA EMI Independent Study Program Web site.
- Select this link to access FEMA National Training and Education Division course catalogs.

Education and Training Resource Examples

A small sample of the education and training resources available through the DHS Office of Infrastructure Protection and the sectors is listed below. Many of the training courses are offered through FEMA's Emergency Management Institute. For more information on DHS-sponsored infrastructure security and resilience education, please contact ip_education@hq.dhs.gov.

DHS Office of Infrastructure Protection Resources

The DHS Office of Infrastructure Protection offers a wide array of training programs and resources, free of charge, to government and private-sector partners.

These classroom and Web-based courses and training resources provide government officials and critical infrastructure owners, operators, and employees with the knowledge and skills needed to identify and implement critical infrastructure security and resilience activities.

Examples of recent security awareness courses developed by the Office of Infrastructure Protection include:

- **Workplace Security Awareness (Independent Study Course IS-906)**
  Provides guidance to individuals and organizations on how to improve security in the workplace. The training illustrates potential security threats such as: access and security control, criminal and suspicious activities, workplace violence, and cyber threats.
- **Active Shooter: What You Can Do (Independent Study Course IS-907)**
  Provides guidance to managers and employees in responding to a situation in which an individual is actively engaged in killing or attempting to kill people in a confined and populated area.
- **Surveillance Awareness: What You Can Do (Independent Study Course IS-914)**
  Provides an overview of surveillance activities and the indicators associated with them, as well as the actions that employees and service providers can take to report potential surveillance incidents.

Sector-Specific Resources

Several sectors offer training programs through FEMA's Emergency Management Institute.

Examples include:

- **Dams Sector: Security Awareness** (FEMA Independent Study Course IS-871, For Official Use Only), which describes common security vulnerabilities, potential indicators of threats, surveillance detection, and reporting of incidents and suspicious activities.
- **Physical Security Criteria for Federal Facilities** (FEMA Independent Study Course IS-892, For Official Use Only), which identifies physical security protective measures to be applied to nonmilitary Federal facilities.

For additional information on sector-specific training, refer to the Sector Overviews portion of the Critical Infrastructure Training Web Page.

Other Education and Training Resources

Private-sector professional and trade associations also provide training and job aids on various industry-related topics involving infrastructure security and resilience.

For example, in the Financial Services Sector:

- The Financial Services – Information Sharing and Analysis Center offers critical infrastructure training and seminars.
- Multiple banking and finance trade associations provide training and job aids on industry-related topics, including the American Bankers Association, the Independent Community Bankers of America, and the Risk Management Association.

Conducting Tests and Exercises

After you have conducted training, you can begin to conduct tests and exercises of the policies and procedures in the security and resilience plan.

Tests and exercises build on the knowledge acquired in the training to:

- Allow testing of critical infrastructure security and resilience policies, plans, and procedures.
- Provide a safe environment to practice procedures using equipment and resources.
- Build relationships that result in better coordination and communication during an incident.

The Office of Infrastructure Protection's Sector-Specific Tabletop Exercise Program provides tools that allow critical infrastructure partners to develop interactive, discussion-based exercises for their communities of interest, at the sector or a facility level. The program allows users to leverage pre-built exercise templates and tailor them to their communities' specific needs in order to assess, develop, and update plans, programs, policies, and procedures within an incident management functional area. For more information, contact the IP Exercise Team at: IP.Exercises@hq.dhs.gov.

Testing Protective Plans, Policies, and Procedures

Testing should be designed to address both:

- Physical protection measures, such as security doors and surveillance cameras.
- Policies and procedures, such as ensuring security doors are not propped open or that security personnel are checking identification for all visitors.

Testing has an added benefit of providing the opportunity to rehearse procedures, such as identifying and responding to an intrusion or responding to a system alert.

Red Teaming

Red teaming, also called red cell teaming and penetration testing, is an effective means of testing protective measures.

Red team members attempt to identify and exploit vulnerabilities in protective measures. For example, an organization may use experts from inside or outside the organization to attempt to bypass its security measures in order to identify potential vulnerabilities. The entity being tested often is unaware in advance of the test.

Conducting and Participating in Exercises

Exercises improve readiness by providing a way to test and evaluate the effectiveness of critical infrastructure security and resilience plans.

Exercises conducted with major stakeholders strengthen critical infrastructure security and resilience capabilities by helping to:

- Improve communications.
- Promote consistency.
- Ensure integration of critical infrastructure security and resilience into preparedness and incident management plans.

Essential Tools

Exercises provide critical infrastructure stakeholders with a set of essential tools to prevent disasters as well as to prepare for, respond to, and recover from them.

Where possible, critical infrastructure security and resilience should be built into other local and regional emergency management and mitigation exercises.

Planning Exercises

Your planning team needs to identify what exercises to conduct and when.

- Begin with exercises that focus on a small part of the plan, or on one specific procedure. Later add more complex exercises.
- Conduct exercises whenever new equipment is purchased or installed, or when new policies or procedures are developed.

Keep in mind that exercises determine how the plan worked, and do not focus on the performance of individuals.

Homeland Security Exercise and Evaluation Program

Exercises assist organizations to develop objective assessments of their capabilities so that strengths and areas for improvement are identified, corrected, and shared as appropriate prior to a real incident.

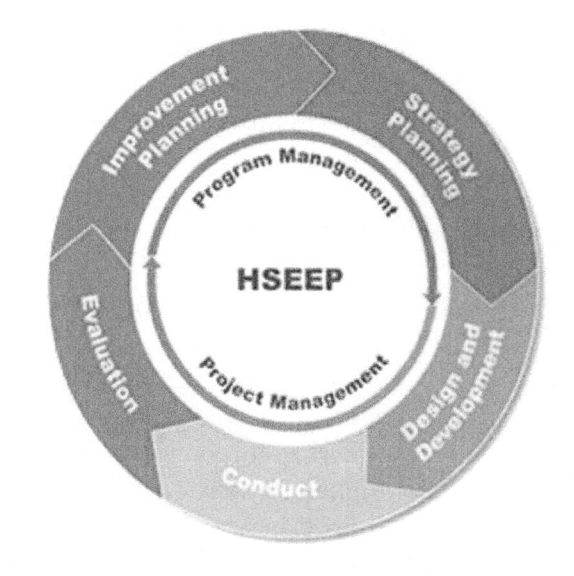

The Homeland Security Exercise and Evaluation Program (HSEEP) provides a set of guiding principles for exercise programs as well as a common methodology for exercise program management, design and development, conduct, evaluation and improvement planning. HSEEP exercise and evaluation doctrine is flexible, scalable and adaptable to the needs of stakeholders across the whole community and is applicable for exercises across all national preparedness mission areas-prevention, protection, mitigation, response and recovery.

HSEEP templates and guidance are available to the whole community and may be accessed at FEMA's exercise webpage.

Selecting Exercises

There are two main categories of exercises:

- **Discussion-based exercises,** which are used to familiarize personnel with procedures and policies. Tabletop exercises are a form of discussion-based exercise.
- **Operations-based exercises,** which are used to validate the plan. These exercises help clarify roles and responsibilities, identify gaps in resources, and improve performance. They include drills, functional exercises, and full-scale exercises.

Tabletop Exercises

A tabletop exercise is a discussion-based activity in which a simulated scenario is presented and participants in the exercise respond as if the scenario were really happening. Tabletop scenarios are often based on actual incidents or recent events in the news, particularly from neighboring or nearby communities.

Tabletops:

- Involve key personnel and emergency responders.
- Allow participants to assess the plan and response procedures.
- Encourage participant discussions, problem-solving, and decisionmaking in a low-stress environment.

Conducting Tabletops

To successfully conduct a tabletop exercise:

- Identify key participants for the exercise.
- Identify facilitator(s) to run the exercise, manage the information exchange, control the discussion, present scenario developments, and guide actions.
- Set exercise goals and objectives to lay out expectations for the exercise. Goals should be measurable and achievable.
- Outline an incident to test a specific set of procedures, capability, and/or policy.

- Conduct a hot wash and a debrief to capture feedback and lessons learned.
- Develop a list of recommendations or an improvement plan to update training and exercise plans.

Drills

Drills are operations-based exercises that usually test a single specific operation or function within a single entity. Conducted in a realistic environment, drills are often used to test new policies or equipment, practice current skills, or prepare for larger scale exercises.

Conducting Drills

To successfully conduct a drill:

- Plans, policies, and procedures must be clearly defined and personnel must be familiar with them.
- Personnel must be trained on the processes and procedures to be drilled.
- It must be clear that a drill is being conducted, and that the situation is not an actual emergency.
- Evaluation and feedback must be included in the drill process.
- First responders should be included.

Using Drills for Simulated Emergencies

Drills can test how well personnel respond to simulated emergencies, including:

- Bomb threats.
- Fires and/or explosions.
- Severe weather, such as a tornado.
- Hazmat incidents, either originating inside or outside a facility.
- Other incidents identified as hazards.

Functional Exercises

A functional exercise is the simulation of an event that:

- Involves various levels of government, owners and operators, and emergency management personnel.
- Involves trained personnel "acting out" their actual roles.
- Evaluates internal capabilities and responses of participants.
- Evaluates the coordination activities between participants.

Full-Scale Exercises

A full-scale exercise is a multiagency, multijurisdictional, multidiscipline operations-based exercise involving functional personnel (e.g., critical infrastructure security and resilience partners) and emergency or other responders (e.g., firefighters decontaminating mock victims).

To test critical infrastructure security and resilience plans using functional or full-scale exercises, planners may wish to inquire about upcoming communitywide exercises. In addition to exercising specific procedures and policies, these large-scale exercises can provide owners and operators with an opportunity to test how their own planning fits into community plans.

Planning Exercises Around Key Concerns

There are several ways to determine the areas in which to focus for critical infrastructure exercises to be held at the local or State level. One recommended method is to focus on key concerns.

Using this method, surveys of critical infrastructure and emergency management experts are used to identify areas of concern.

For example, if a key concern is the interaction between the public and private sectors, an exercise testing communications and decisionmaking policies and plans might identify ways to improve these interactions in advance of a crisis.

Planning Exercises Around Highest Priority Assets and Systems

Exercise designers also could focus exercises on the highest priority assets and systems.

For example, an exercise could test how the failure of electrical power affects key assets and systems. Such an exercise might indicate:

- Whether there are gaps in security and resilience, such as ensuring that trained operators and repair personnel are available to restore power.
- Where backup power is required while electrical power is restored.
- How necessary decisions are made and communicated.

Planning Exercises Around Threats/Hazards and Consequences

Another method of identifying the focus of a planned exercise is to use the threat/hazard assessment worksheet from the previous module to identify the highest probability threats/hazards and the greatest consequences.

As explained in the worksheet, the need to exercise for frequent and low-consequence threats/hazards may be less important. Prioritization for training and exercising should be risk-informed.

Exercise Design Courses

The FEMA EMI Independent Study program offers several courses on exercise planning, design, and evaluation, including:

- IS-120.a, An Introduction to Exercises.
- IS-130, Exercise Evaluation and Improvement Planning.
- IS-139, Exercise Design.

Select this link to access the FEMA EMI Independent Study Program Web site.

Exercise Evaluation

Exercise evaluation is an important component of testing and exercising.

The focus of evaluation should be on how well the policies, plans, and procedures worked.

The results of the evaluation, including lessons learned, should be incorporated into an after-action report.

Documenting Lessons Learned

The next step of the continuous improvement process is to document the lessons learned from testing and exercising, as well as from actual threats and hazards.

Lessons learned always should be identified in an after-action report. This document serves as the basis for:

- Planning future training and exercises.
- Revising policies, plans, and procedures.
- Taking other corrective actions, such as purchase of equipment that is compatible across several jurisdictions.

After-Action Recommendations and Corrective Actions

The format of the after-action report depends on the needs and requirements of the jurisdiction. To ensure continuous improvement, after-action reports should include recommendations for improvement and identify corrective actions.

The following are common elements of after-action reports:

Element	Description
Statement of the Problem	A description of the reason the exercise was conducted.
Exercise Summary	Includes information such as: - The exercise objectives. - A list of the players and organizations. - A brief description of the exercise scenario.
Strengths and Areas for Improvement	Based on feedback from:

	<ul><li>Exercise player feedback.</li><li>Evaluator assessment.</li><li>After-action review findings.</li></ul>
Recommendations and Corrective Actions	Includes recommendations and corrective actions concerning:<ul><li>Training needs.</li><li>Changes required to policies, plans, and procedures.</li><li>Needed resources (human, physical, and fiscal).</li></ul>

Taking Corrective Actions

The next step for ensuring continuous improvement is to take corrective actions.

There is little value to testing and exercising security and resilience programs and documenting lessons learned unless corrective actions are implemented.

The measure of success is whether organizations make improvements and are better prepared to respond to and recover from crises.

Continuous Improvement

Training is a key component of ensuring continuous improvement.

Corrective actions that are documented in lessons learned or after-action reports may include or require additional or enhanced training.

Training also may be required to implement new or enhanced plans, policies, and procedures based on the results of exercises or incidents.

Training and exercising form a continuous loop with corrective actions to ensure improvement.

Implementation Plans

Results of an after-action report are translated into strategies for making corrections in an implementation plan. A corrective implementation plan should include:

- Specific actions that must be taken, including revisions to policies, plans, and procedures; training; additional exercises; and other actions (for example, the purchase of new equipment).
- The expected outcomes from the corrective actions.
- The organizations/persons responsible for the corrective actions.
- The schedule by which the actions must be completed.

Add or Update Plans

After corrective actions are identified in implementation plans, the relevant policies, plans, and procedures for critical infrastructure security and resilience should be added or updated as necessary.

Exercise planners should ensure that lessons learned and corrective actions from other exercises – such as emergency management and predisaster mitigation exercises – also are incorporated into critical infrastructure security and resilience planning as needed.

Resources

Select the links below for additional information relating to the content of this lesson.

Lesson Resources

- Common Elements of After-Action Reports
- Critical Infrastructure Security and Resilience Activities Checklists
- Education and Training Resource Examples
- Exercise Categories
- HSEEP 2013

Training Courses

- IS-120.a, An Introduction to Exercises
- IS-130, Exercise Evaluation and Improvement Planning
- IS-906, Workplace Security Awareness
- IS-907, Active Shooter: What You Can Do

Web Pages

- Critical Infrastructure Security Web site
- Critical Infrastructure Resources
- Critical Infrastructure Training
- Federal Emergency Management Agency's Emergency Management Institute (EMI) Independent Study Courses
- Federal Emergency Management Agency's National Training and Education Division Courses
- Homeland Security Exercise and Evaluation Program (HSEEP)
- Lessons Learned Information Sharing
- Office of Infrastructure Protection (DHS) Web Site

Lesson Summary

In this lesson, you learned about ensuring continuous improvement by testing and exercising critical infrastructure security and resilience programs.

Made in United States
North Haven, CT
01 February 2022